Approaching Sociology

THE STUDENTS LIBRARY OF SOCIOLOGY

GENERAL EDITOR: ROY EMERSON

Professor of Sociology
University of East Anglia

Approaching Sociology: a Critical Introduction

Margaret A. Coulson
Senior Lecturer in Sociology, Harris College, Preston

David S. Riddell
Lecturer in Sociology, University of Lancaster

LONDON
ROUTLEDGE & KEGAN PAUL

First published 1970
by Routledge & Kegan Paul Ltd
Broadway House, 68-74 Carter Lane
London, E.C.4
Printed in Great Britain by
Northumberland Press Limited
Gateshead
ISBN 0 7100 6877 8 (c)
ISBN 0 7100 6878 6 (p)

Contents

CONTENTS

General Editor's introduction

Today Sociology is going through a phase of great expansion. Not only is there a widespread general interest in the subject, but there is a rapid growth in the numbers of new courses at Universities, Colleges of Further Education, and elsewhere. As a result there is an increasing number of potential readers of introductory textbooks. Some will be motivated by general interest; some will want to find out enough about the subject to see whether they would like to pursue a formal course in it; and others will already be following courses into which an element of Sociology has been fused. One approach to these readers is by means of the comprehensive introductory volume giving a general coverage of the field of Sociology; another is by means of a series of monographs each providing an introduction to a selected topic. Both these approaches have their advantages and disadvantages. The *Library of Sociology* adopts the second approach. It will cover a more extensive range of topics than could be dealt with in a single volume; while at the same time each volume will provide a thorough introductory treatment of any one topic. The reader who has little or no knowledge in the field will find within any particular book a foundation upon which to build, and to extend by means of the suggestions for further reading.

Anyone who has taught introductory Sociology courses will know that two major problems present themselves. The first is to explain what is after all a very complicated subject in a way which is comprehensible to the beginning student. The second is to maintain the student's interest. Many people approach the study of Sociology for the first time because they have an interest in the current problems of society and they believe that such a study will provide them with a relevant basis for the understanding of those problems. Of course all sociologists do believe that the study of their subject is relevant to such an understanding. It nevertheless is regrettably true that many introductions to the subject and in particular many introductory textbooks present their arguments in ways which must leave the reader to ask how all this is relevant to the social milieu in which he finds himself.

The present volume meets both these points. It approaches the subject matter in simple and direct language while at the same time the reader becomes acquainted with important—and controversial—issues central to sociological analysis. The authors themselves are concerned to make clear that 'this book is not itself intended on its own as a textbook of sociology but is rather meant to be used in conjunction with other introductory material to provide the basis of a critique'. The reader of the volume will not find an eclectic approach. The authors are committed to a dialectical analysis of society. Their approach may be compared and contrasted with other approaches to the subject.

At the present time, the available techniques and models of analysis within sociology are being subjected to much re-examination and searching criticism. The criteria by which they can be evaluated are unclear. It is therefore all the more important to demonstrate to the interested inquirer that the choice is not to be made in terms of personal predilection but in terms of the effectiveness with which these techniques and models can provide an understanding of societies. The reader should be stimulated by the clear and incisive statement in this book to investigate for himself the important issues raised in it.

A. R. EMERSON

1
Sociology as a critical discipline

The diversity of views in sociology

All over the world, people starting to learn about physics, or any other of the natural sciences, will be learning very much the same sorts of things. The same sets of basic propositions will be learnt in Japan and Russia, China and Peru. But this is not true in sociology. The student in Russia will not start off with the same propositions about societies and men's relation to them as the student in the U.S.A. The British student and the Yugoslav student will not be learning the same sorts of propositions to start off their studies (Aron, 1968, p. 7f.). More than this, even within a country, to a considerable extent the approach which a student finds he is being taught varies according to the particular views of his teacher or his department. In Canada, for example, two distinct traditions of sociology exist side by side: French Canadian, drawing from European and especially French sociology, and English Canadian, which follows one or other of the American schools (Bottomore, 1967, p. 112-113). In some places the diversity of views on the subject will be emphasized, in others it will be ignored, or underplayed. No doubt there will be some elements in common in most of the courses students will be taking across the world, but these will, in fact, be very largely restricted to the study of such things as technical means of carrying out surveys of opinion and attitude, around which a certain amount of technology has developed. Among sociologists there are different reactions to the problem of the diversity of approaches and orientations. It will tell us something of what sociology is about if we examine them.

For some sociologists, the problem is relatively simple. Since *their* approach is right, and those of other schools wrong, the latter can safely be ignored. It is very easy to see this if we compare basic textbooks of sociology from different countries—the kind of contents that they list, the kind of authors they consider important, the kind of orientations that they adopt. Here are some examples. There are large numbers of American textbooks, well-produced, very lengthy (in no country are there so many students of sociology as there are in the United States). Almost all of them orient their approach to sociology around the concept of *culture*, which we shall discuss later. But if we look at European textbooks, we find them giving much less emphasis to the idea of culture, and emphasizing much more the idea of *structure*. Similarly, in most American, and in a number of British textbooks, the idea of social change is given a very subordinate place —sometimes a chapter is 'tacked on' to a book—whereas all East European textbooks give a central place to the concept of change. George Gurvitch, one of the great French sociologists (although we do not agree with his sociological approach in general), calls Marx the 'Prince of Sociologists', and Marx's work is basic to the approach of large numbers of East European sociologists; yet he is not even given the dignity of a section in Barnes' 1000-page *Introduction to the History of Sociology*, and hardly, if at all, mentioned in most of the American introductory texts (Barnes, 1961). While most of the latter depend almost entirely on the *functionalist* orientation to sociology, in Bottomore's textbook, which is one of the most widely used (and, in our view, best) textbooks in Britain, this orientation is dismissed in a few lines (Bottomore, 1963). Yet, if one's reading were confined to the approach of one of the particular schools mentioned, one would hardly even know that other approaches existed, and were widely held elsewhere. We think it is unfortunate that this applies to very many students of the subject, whose orientation is implicitly selected for them before they begin.

A comparison of an American and a Yugoslav textbook of sociology

Leonard Broom & Philip Selznick *Sociology*, 3rd. edition, 1963	Ante Fiamengo *Elements of General Sociology* 5th. edition, 1967
Part 1 Elements of Sociological Analysis	Introduction
Ch. 1 Introduction	Ch. 1 Historical Development of Sociological Thought—the Sources of Sociology
Ch. 2 Social Organization	
Ch. 3 Culture	
Ch. 4 Socialization	
Ch. 5 Primary Groups	Ch. 2 The Origin of Sociology as a Separate Science
Ch. 6 Social Stratification	
Ch. 7 Associations	Ch. 3 The Object and Method of Sociology
Ch. 8 Collective Behaviour	
Ch. 9 Population and Ecology	Ch. 4 The Basic Ideas of Sociology
	Ch. 5 The Structure and Dialectics of Forces and Relations of Production
Part 2 Analysis of Special Areas	
Ch. 10 The Family	Ch. 6 Society as a Totality

3

Quite a difference! Notice that even from the chapter headings you can see that Broom and Selznick's emphasis is static, while Fiamengo's is dynamic; Fiamengo's structuralist, while B. & S. emphasize culture and socialization. We should say that a comparison of the total contents of the two books bear out the differences in the contents' lists.

Another justification of the limitations which authors impose on the knowledge they presume to allow the student of sociology is that the 'theoretical' problems are too difficult for a beginning student to grasp; he needs a firm base before he can tackle these more difficult questions. This would be acceptable, perhaps, if there was indeed a 'firm base', which had been solidly established, examples have already been given to indicate that this is not the case. The argument is therefore spurious.

An alternative approach, again popular in American textbooks, is to argue that sociology is a science, just like the natural sciences, but at a much less developed level; therefore evaluations and controversy should be avoided in the introductory stages. If, however, we

4

examine these books in a comparative way, we find that, although sociology clearly is undeveloped when compared with the natural sciences in terms of the amount of effort, resources, and time given to research, what *has* been done has not led to a body of agreement which we can be sure that everybody accepts. While sociologists will not dispute that x per cent of people have a particular opinion on some subject at a particular time when asked a certain question, what this *means* in terms of their behaviour, in terms of theories about the explanation of behaviour in society, *will* be in dispute (see Chapter 6). In addition to this, the proponents of such a view are unable to match up to the scientific criteria they set themselves. For example, in Horton and Hunt's *Sociology* (1964), the first chapter tells us about the scientific nature of sociology, that it abjures value judgments, unverifiable and unsubstantiated statements, etc., yet the authors find themselves able later on to describe the Soviet Union as an 'unparalleled tyranny'. Inkeles, in *What is Sociology?* (1964), after similar obeisance to the god of Science, concludes his book with a section which reads: 'The United States is viewed by most peoples of the world as dynamic and progressive to a degree which they hardly can imagine, and certainly do not expect to realize, for their own countries,' (p. 112). Over and above this, the scientific methods used, despite their apparent sophistication, are often inappropriate to the problems.

The argument so far leads up to the proposition that we should regard with considerable distrust anyone who tries to tell us that there is *an* approach to sociology which we should learn alone, that there is *really* a considerable amount of agreement about most things, so that we needn't bother about the argument. The effect is to lull the critical faculties of the student—who often finds it difficult enough to cope with the amount of new knowledge anyway —and to make it easier for the teacher to put across

5

his approach, or that of *his* school of sociology, without challenge. It can be confidently asserted that the interpretation of almost any piece of social evidence is controversial as between different sociological schools. No approach to the study of sociology which does not emphasize this fact should be acceptable. A second important line of argument follows from the first. Since there is no agreed base, from the beginning the sociology student has to make judgments about, and interpretations of, the various propositions that he is introduced to. It is impossible to make such judgments on an *ad hoc* basis, and it is essential to have some kind of broader theoretical perspective which integrates material, and provides criteria by which to evaluate problems. In our view, the choice of such a perspective is not something arbitrary —tweedledum or tweedledee—but develops as a student relates different approaches to different problems and implicitly compares them. Nor should a perspective or approach be held in an absolute manner—or we should be dealing with a theology, not a social science. Yet many introductory textbooks ignore the need to inform the student of the perspectives available for him to choose from. Instead we are given selections from a range of the various areas that sociologists have studied—urban sociology, industrial sociology, sociology of crime and delinquency, sociology of education, socialization, and so on; selections which are made on the basis of the perspectives of the author, who nowhere gives the student the opportunity to judge these perspectives themselves by laying them out in contrast to those of other sociologists. Again the big American textbooks are most guilty on this score, but some of the British ones are almost equally bad (e.g. Cotgrove, 1967, who indicates some of the problems in his first chapter, without apparently realizing their fundamental importance). We have our own views as to the most appropriate sort of perspective for sociologists, and put it forward in this book, because we think that an introductory book ought to do this. We also try to introduce some other perspectives critically, and give references so that students may, by additional reading, make judgments as to their relative helpfulness.

Sociologists as People

There are therefore very big disagreements among sociologists about orientations to the subject, and about the attitude that should be taken to the disagreements themselves. Why is this? Obviously it is in part due to differences of assessment of certain theories and actual studies, and it is with argument about these that the later parts of the book are concerned, but the problem is itself also a sociological one. Sociologists, and, to a greater or lesser degree, other social scientists, face two important kinds of problems in their work. Firstly, the propositions that they make are about people—how they are affected by belonging to certain kinds of groups, indeed, more than this, that people are inconceivable without groups. Mannheim, a famous sociologist, put it thus :

> We belong to a group not only because we are born into it, not merely because we confess to belong to it, nor finally because we give it our loyalty and allegiance, but primarily because we see the world and certain things in the world the way it does (Mannheim, 1960, p. 19).

But sociologists are also people, are therefore also members of groups, and, in as far as the above statement is true, will also tend to see the world in the way the groups they belong to do. Therefore we should expect to learn something about what sociologists say as socio-

from pt of view of cud/wied of group

logists by studying the nature of the different kinds of groups they belong to. (We are using the word group in a very general sense here, and not simply thinking of people meeting together face to face.)

There has been some objection to this kind of approach on the grounds that it lands one in what is called an infinite regression—the person making the analysis of the effect on sociologists of being in groups himself belongs to groups; thus his analysis could itself be analysed in the same terms, and so on ad infinitum. Philosophically, the point is true, but, in practice, the possibility of an infinite regression does not allow us to ignore the problem. Some studies in social psychology have shown that, even under apparently very careful designs, the attitudes and expectations of the investigators have marked effects on the results (Rosenthal, 1966). Why then should the problem be ignored in sociology, or indeed in real life, where such rigour of experiment can, for various reasons, never hold?

The second problem for sociologists is that their subject matter is inextricably bound up with the kinds of problems the solution of which concerns every human being in one way or another; over which vast, continent-wide disagreements exist; for which many have died—such problems as war and peace, socialism, poverty, unemployment, the relations between men and women, and so on. To investigate them involves sociologists in great historical arguments, and makes it very difficult for them to divorce their own views as citizens from their work as sociologists. Some sociologists have tried to evade this problem by resolutely refusing to study anything that might conceivably have social significance (c.f. Moore, 1963). But this is really no escape, since even the decision as to what to study or what not to study is a social decision and can be judged in moral terms: 'By their work, all students of man and society assume and imply moral and political decisions.' (Mills, 1959, p. 76.) Thus, to a greater or lesser degree, in various ways, the sociologist cannot avoid the problem of social values in his work. We do not think that the first and second problems are totally separable, since one of our basic propositions is that values and ideas are not independent of the groups, and relations between groups in which people find themselves, although this doesn't mean that they are considered to be totally determined by them. The problem is analysed further in Chapter 5.

On the basis of these two related problems for sociologists, let us therefore return to the fact that there is no basic agreement among sociologists in different societies with different social structures, and even within societies, and that they so often try to hide or play down or 'leave until later' this uncomfortable fact. We can pose it this way: what are some of the characteristics of the sorts of groups that sociologists belong to? (c.f. Horowitz, 1968.) Since this is a general sociological question, it applies to more groups than sociologists alone, and in our discussion we shall, in fact, be raising propositions which can help us to understand how sociology should approach the study of other social problems. Because our discussion is not intended as a systematic analysis of the 'sociology of sociologists', it is phrased in very general terms, and will not enable us to predict the behaviour of individual sociologists (see below p. 15).

Let us start off at a very general level, that of whole societies. Those groups who have effective control of a society may propose that only certain forms of approach or theory are proper, and may be prepared to enforce their view with violence or threats to the security of the sociologist. Thus, in fascist Germany, sociologists were required to work within a framework of racialist myths so intolerable that most of them felt obliged to leave (Neumann, 1966). Antonio Gramsci, perhaps the leading

Italian thinker, spent ten years of his life in the jail where he eventually died (Merrington, 1968). For many years, sociology was not an acceptable discipline in the Soviet Union, and at the time of writing the works of one of the greatest Soviet social analysts, Leon Trotsky, are not available to students there.

Or there may be more subtle means of control. In the United States, an enquiry in 1955 by Lazarsfeld and Thielens, conducted on a sample of nearly 2,500 social science teachers, found that very nearly one quarter censored their own teaching so as to avoid difficulties, and 40 per cent were concerned less 'warped' versions of what they said were passed on by students. More than two thirds of those in the bigger institutions of high academic repute knew of at least one incident involving attacks on colleagues for their views or associations (Lazarsfeld and Thielens, 1958). Thus, strong pressures may be exerted by those controlling societies, in some cases more directly, in some cases in a more roundabout way, for sociology to be taught in a certain way, for some approaches to be emphasized at the expense of others (Birnbaum, 1958). If we continue to consider the United States, and we wish to do so, since the influence of its sociology is a dominant one in Britain, the development of teaching in sociology since the Second World War cannot be divorced from the confrontation between that country (and its allies), and the Soviet Union (and its allies). While it would be a crude over simplification to say that the general prevalence of theories emphasizing order, stability, and the maintenance of the status quo (functionalism), was a result of a demand for an ideology to provide a weapon in the struggle against Soviet 'socialism', it would be even more crudely mistaken to believe that this type of theory developed entirely as a result of independent reflection (Aron, 1968, introduction, Cohn-Bendit, 1969).

Coercion and pressure are, then, more or less important to sociologists in different societies at different historical periods. But what of the students of a teacher who practises self-censorship in one form or another? What was deliberate distortion on his part will appear a natural approach to them, and they, when they begin to influence others, will not be censoring themselves in expressing censored views—they don't know that biases are incorporated in their approach. It may be objected that the teaching of sociology is not a simple matter of passing on information (or lack of it) from one generation to the next, that there are other influences. This is true, but let us suppose that most of these other influences tend to work in the same way; in that case the biases presented by the original teacher would be reinforced. Thus, if we call all the factors together going to make the new sociologist, his *socialization*, and if all those factors reinforce a similar bias, then that bias comes to be seen not as a bias, but as the obvious, sensible, reasonable, scientific approach. This is one way in which schools of sociology, and social ideologies in general, are developed.

Let us consider therefore some of the other factors. There is a famous study by Bettleheim of the behaviour of the inmates of a Nazi concentration camp (Bettleheim, 1943). So adaptable are human beings that many prisoners, under the extreme pressure of the life in the camp, came to believe that they really were the despicable scum of the earth that the guards thought they were. In sociological jargon, they internalized the standards of the guards about themselves. A sociologist is not subject to such extreme pressures; but neither is what may be demanded of him so serious in its implications for his self-esteem. Thus for every sociologist who censored himself in the U.S. enquiry referred to, we can be sure that there were others, many others, who did not need self-censorship, because nothing that they said would be likely to disturb anyone—they had come to define sociology in terms which would not cause trouble. If we generalize this point to other situations, and indeed to whole societies, as Marcuse has quite legitimately done, it creates immense problems in defining what people's *real* beliefs are, problems discussed in Chapter 5 (Marcuse, 1964).

We have talked about pressures on sociologists to teach in certain ways, emphasize certain approaches to the exclusion of others, and about how these are transmitted —either by coercion, internalization, or adoption over generations (of sociologists). It is also important that groups of people in different types of occupations differ in their attitudes, and in their standard and mode of life from those in other types. The explanation of these differences is a crucial question for sociology—all too often they are just described. In our class societies, socio-logists are very definitely middle class. Let us consider the British situation. The established teaching sociologist in University or College moves in a restricted and comfort-able world. His employment is secure and well paid, with steady rises in income—apart from certain minor anxiety periods at job changes—until retirement, or near it. He has rather comfortable working conditions, long holidays, and a more comfortable house in the suburbs of a fairly large urban centre. Of course, not only sociologists, but all college and university teachers are in more or less this position, and their social attitudes reflect it. Those with a conscience tend to wish everyone could live like them, and the others worry about groups which might conceiv-ably be a threat to them in some way or another (like students in the present period). Such a background, the atmosphere and associations deriving from it, would tend to make certain kinds of social theory seem more appro-priate than others, while certain standards of politesse develop—*norms* of appropriate behaviour in the jargon—

which lead to some types of argument being disparaged because of the 'rough' language in which they are expressed, their polemical style, or because of their author's 'dubious' connections, rather than because of their content (e.g. Lipset and Smelser, 1961, footnote 12). In the United States, where job security is less certain until the higher reaches of the academic world, pressure to conform to certain norms is reinforced by the local power wielded by those in a position to confirm or deny appointments, a situation which has been ably studied by Caplow and McGhee in their book *The Academic Marketplace* (1961). If there are pressures on sociologists not to countenance theories or behaviour that might lead to deviation from norms of academic propriety deriving from the social position and relationships of academics, pressures also develop among the sociologists themselves. For sociologists, in this country at least, have only recently and tentatively arrived at positions of academic respectability in the eyes of their longer established colleagues, and thus they are often like *nouveaux riches*, trying to establish the power of their departments, their status in academic institutions. This situation leads to an emphasis on the 'real' unity of the discipline, the *consensus* (amount of agreement as to norms) of the discipline, the professional qualities of sociologists, and their ability to make 'positive' contributions to the administration of things as they are. It leads away from an emphasis on disagreement, and the sort of theory which argues that problems derive from the fact that things are as they are, i.e., that the social organization itself needs changing if the problems are to be solved. Over and above this, there is a tendency for sociologists to become so absorbed in establishing themselves in the eyes of other sociologists whom they esteem (their *reference groups*), that the relationship between what they do and social reality can become very tenuous indeed. Some of the arguments about sociological arguments seem to the authors to have a very great resemblance to the medieval disputations as to the number of angels that could be accommodated on the head of a pin. Compare, for instance, Hoselitz (1966), Sosensky (1964), Zollschan and Perucci (1964) with the devastating critique by Frank (1967b).

What we have done is to set out some of the pressures that we can expect to be exerted upon sociologists as teachers because of the fact that they are members of certain groups, and how these pressures may be reinforced through time. Let us summarize them. By belonging to a society with a certain type of social structure (e.g. capitalist, communist), they may be *coerced* in certain ways. More subtle pressures may lead them to adapt themselves by adopting as their own internalizing the demands made upon them. Succeeding generations may be so *socialized* that they will be less aware that choices are available. Within the society, because of their membership of certain occupational groups, sociologists are constantly pressured to approach their studies from the perspective of these groups; by adopting current *norms* giving high values to personal social advancement, for example, they are pressured not to behave in ways which might offend those in positions above them, in order to secure their own advancement. Finally, by belonging to a local academic group of sociologists, they are pressured to adjust themselves to that which will gain them esteem in the eyes of the majority of that group—or the opinion formers, the influentials, within it.

This, then, is a general sociological approach by which we can begin to explain why whole schools of sociologists systematically misinform their students as to the extent of the diversity of approaches that exist within the rubric of the term sociology. We think it is sociological, because it tries to relate behaviour and attitudes to the kinds of social groups that sociologists belong to.

The same *kind* of analysis, we think, is a basis for the sociological study of all behaviour and attitudes, i.e., it tells us how a sociologist should set about approaching problems. If he wants to understand why *you* behave and think as you do, this is the way the sociologist should begin to set about it. You will find this type of analysis in all the examples that we give. But two further points should be mentioned.

Firstly, this kind of approach does not tell us that every sociologist subject to similar influences will behave in the same way—such a crude determinism has been very frequent in social theories, and leads to endless struggling as the theorists seek to escape self-made problems, when people don't behave as they 'ought to'. It does seek to help us to understand types of behaviour generally existing among groups of people who call themselves sociologists, no more. The other point is related to the first. Since no narrow determinism is involved, a sociologist who becomes aware that these pressures are affecting his approach, can, if he wishes, alter the situation somewhat—either by changing the group affiliations that he has, or by trying to compensate for his group affiliations. In the opinion of the authors, neither of these methods is likely to be more effective than relentless criticism from knowledgeable students—but how to stimulate this? The point in general does not only apply to the example given, but can be generalized. We think that the purpose of sociology is not to build a closed system of determinate laws, but by scientific study, to enable people to become aware of some of the social reasons for the social problems that they experience, to be able to direct their attention to appropriate sorts of remedies for them. It can also help them to understand themselves better.

Our criticisms in this chapter of the way sociologists often teach are not meant to be attacks on the value of studying the subject of sociology, but are one half of an argument as to why even the first year student needs a critical approach to what he is taught.

> If we would teach students how science is made, really made rather than as publicly reported, we cannot fail to expose them to the whole scientist by whom it is made, with all his gifts and blindnesses, with all his methods as well. To do otherwise is to usher in an era of spiritless technicians who will be no less lacking in understanding than they are in passion, and who will be useful only because they can be used (Gouldner, 1963).

The second half of this argument comes in Chapters 3, 4 and 5.

Society

One of the 'groups' that we talked of in discussing the problem of sociologists and their subject was society. It is worth having a further look at this term, and terms related to it, because they have been, and are, the source of endless confusion among sociologists and others. Sociologists are always talking about society, but very few of them bother to define it satisfactorily. In some of the huge 'scientific' American textbooks of the subject, there is no definition at all.

In common usage, 'society' can refer to a small group formed for some purpose—a learned society, a student political society, and so on—but sociologists don't use it in this meaning. The term is also sometimes used in a very vague and general sense to denote a huge region with some common cultural or organizational feature—e.g., Western society. But usually we mean a nation state when we talk of a society. If we talk about Indian society, or Zulu society, or British society, we are referring to the whole collection of things, people and goings-on within the boundaries of India, Zululand or Britain. It is very easy to go on from this to make a very serious kind of mistake. It is one thing to explain the behaviour of some-one in terms of the pressures caused by being a member of a society organized in a certain way, but it is quite another to say that the society caused the behaviour. It is very tempting to do this, as a sort of shorthand, but the result is an impression that there is an odd sort of thing—society, over and above the individuals and things, and their organization, in a nation. This seems silly enough when presented in this way, and is called the error of agelicism or reification, treating as an object something which is not an object (Berger and Pullberg, 1966, Blackburn, 1969, p. 206f.). Nevertheless, it is very common, and some famous sociologists, (notably Emile Durkheim, who some seventy years ago had constantly to wage a battle against people who said that the way people behaved wasn't related at all to the way the societies they belonged to were organized) often give the impres-sion that some mystical entity, society itself, was a cause of people's behaviour (Benoit-Smullyan, 1961). Here are some examples from sociology books to show how this 'shorthand' can confuse things:

Often society becomes the initiator rather than the location of some activity or pattern of organization:

Every society controls to some extent who may mate with whom (Goode, 1964).

The more the idea is developed, the more confusing it becomes. For example, Berger (1963, p. 112) compares the relationship between individual and society to that between actor and playwright:

We can say that society provides the script for all the dramatis personae. The individual actors, therefore, need but slip into the roles already assigned to them before the curtain goes up. As long as they play their roles as provided for in the script the social play can proceed as planned.

So 'society' 'plans', 'writes' and 'assigns' the parts we play! The metaphor may be introduced to emphasize the importance of social influences on our behaviour, but this personification of society prevents us from developing any understanding of the actual sources of these influences or of their interplay; everything is masked by what 'society' does or says. This criticism is developed further on page 38.

Inkeles (1964, p. 35) describes the main concern of one of the influential schools of sociologists, the structural functionalists, as being an attempt:

> to delineate the conditions and demands of social life, and to trace the process whereby a given society arranges to meet its needs. To choose an obvious example, if a society is to continue, it must periodically find new members. In all known societies the need is met by some form of family system. The family is the institution which 'acts' for society to ensure fulfillment of the functions of sexual reproduction, of early care of the dependent infant, and of his initial training in the ways of the society in which he will live.

Perhaps this rather bizarre picture of 'society' periodically noticing that it needs some new recruits and setting up families to produce and mould these to the appropriate specifications, is near enough to caricature to require no further comment; we shall discuss this sort of sociology more fully in Chapter 3. You will be able to find many more examples like these in sociological literature and in common usage.

Often the use in this way of a word denoting a collection of people or things can become a substitute for having to think out the real nature of the problem, as it is with the word society for a lot of sociologists, and sociology students, too. Vulgar Marxists are often very guilty of this. The 'Ruling Class', or the 'Bureaucracy' are often held responsible for all social ills, but the actual nature of these groups in specific social situations isn't defined. The approach is very attractive because it enables some-one to explain the problems of any society in a simple formula without having to bother to examine the society itself. This kind of 'analysis' once made Marx himself say in exasperation, 'I am not a Marxist', and the presence of such crudity is the best indication that the analysis is not, in fact, a Marxist one. But it is not only vulgar Marxists who make this sort of mistake. In our societies, politicians constantly justify their actions in terms of the 'National Interest'—to have an incomes policy is in the National Interest, to make atomic weapons is in the National Interest, and so on. If we think about it for a moment, the difficulty of defining what really is a 'national interest' is immense. Almost every policy deci-sion affects some groups in a nation more adversely than others. Thus, to say that a decision is in the national interest usually means to identify the interests of one group of the population with the national interest, while conveniently forgetting the interests of those members of the nation who are not benefited by the decision. By the appeal to nationalism, sectional decisions may appear more palatable to those they *don't* benefit. Finally, there is the constant reference to anyone in control, anyone who does things, as 'they'. 'They' are mending the road, 'they' are building a block of flats, and, more importantly, 'they' as opposed to 'us', control decisions in industry, in politics, and in every relationship that people have with official-dom. These latter forms of expression have been considered to be characteristic of the way working class people look at the world (Gouldthorpe and Lockwood, 1963). If the incorrect use of terms such as society, the bureaucracy, and the national interest can serve to confuse people as to the real nature of interest groups involved in decisions, so can this dichotomous agelicism into 'us' and 'them' indicate that people feel apart, alien from the sources of decisions, and is, or should be, a matter of concern for people in any form of society which is supposed to be democratic (Riddell, 1968, p. 65).

In this chapter we have not tried to explain directly what sociology is. Rather, we have tried to present a critique and explanation in sociological terms of the one-sided, partial nature of the explanations that students very often receive as to what sociology is. Because we have treated all this in what we consider a sociological way, we have been able to introduce some of the jargon commonly found among, and endlessly accumulated by, sociologists, and some of the problems which the explanation of behaviour in terms of groups raises; especially the dangers of treating societies, or equivalent terms for conglomerations of people and things, as if they represent real entities. It has emerged that our idea of what sociology is, what distinguishes it from other disciplines, lies in the way sociologists approach the explanation of phenomena or problems, by seeking causes for them in the facts of people's membership of social groups and in the ways in which these groups are related to each other. This is a simple idea, but there are various reasons why it isn't very easy to explain—we have found—to people in our own society. In the next chapter we shall try to sketch some of these reasons, and explore more aspects of the importance of group membership.

2

The individual and society

Resistances to sociological explanation

Having introduced sociology to students for some six years, and remembering back to our own days as students starting a sociology course, there is no doubt in our minds that many students find it difficult to get hold of the manner of approach to the study of human behaviour that, in our view, is characteristic of sociology, namely that in terms of group membership, and group organization. Apart from vague feelings of rootlessness because of the seeming amorphousness of the subject, dissatisfaction is usually expressed in terms of two specific arguments. Firstly, that since every individual is different, explanation of individuals in terms of groups is impossible. This argument contains a logical fallacy, as we shall try to demonstrate below. The second argument is that this kind of explanation is contrary to the doctrine of free will; with this we have some sympathy, although not in the religious terms in which it is usually formulated. Before considering these arguments themselves, it is worth asking whether there are any features of the socialization of students who take sociology themselves which might lead them towards these views, which often seem to us to be ideologies, partial self-justifications, rather than

21

rational arguments. We can put the problem this way. What are the pressures which are brought to bear on the prospective sociology student before he comes to the institution where he learns sociology?

If we compare societies organized like our own on the basis of capitalist, private property relationships, with feudal societies or some of the undeveloped (economically) societies studied by anthropologists, the emphasis on individualism, individual achievement, individual responsibility, is very marked. In various ways this has been noted by the great sociologists of the past. For instance, Max Weber argued that without such an individualist ethic, capitalism could not have developed (Weber, 1965, Tawney, 1948). Nowadays, the controllers of large sections of the press—both editors, and those who are in a position to exert pressure on them—and of political opinion define success in terms of individual achievement. For the student who will be taking sociology, the way the education system is organized expresses this in practical ways. For instance, co-operation in schools is usually defined as 'cheating' and discouraged. In school classes individuals are constantly examined for their achievement in different subjects, and ranked against one another. It is also true that there are counter currents to this individualism. They stem from the fact that for the workers in a society based on private property ownership, individualism historically provided no protection, and any improvements in wages and conditions, whether on economic or political level, have always come from collective action, rather than from isolated individuals, who found themselves powerless. It is not surprising therefore that young people who have been brought up in workers' families have considerable problems of adjustment to the way things are done in the 'upper' levels of the traditional education system, as Jackson and Marsden's study of working class boys in a grammar school has indicated (Jackson and Marsden, 1962). The prevalence of individualism means that some of the things that sociologists talk about seem to be a challenge to the whole way of thinking that many students have developed through the period of their previous secondary education, and are resisted much more strongly than would otherwise be the case. The idea is often expressed in tutorial groups that people are 'naturally' competitive, or 'naturally' selfish, although it is very easy to show by the use of examples from anthropology that the degree of selfishness or competitiveness that people exhibit depends on the organization of the society from which they come. The frequency with which this sort of argument is linked with denunciations of communism, or assertions to the effect that a 'classless' society is impossible, indicates that students very often feel that some justification of 'their' society, of 'their' way of life, is involved in such arguments, as, in a certain sense, it may very well be.

'Every individual is different', or, 'Every individual is unique, therefore he can't be explained sociologically'. Let us examine this very common argument against sociological types of explanation. We can look at it in two ways. If it were followed to its logical conclusion it would mean that we could never make any predictions about how anyone would behave. For example, when we go into a café, we are pretty sure that there will be someone to cook the food, and someone to serve it (barring self-service cafés). If people, in spite of being individuals, did not behave as others expected them to, at least sometimes, the whole of life would be impossible. The statements that sociologists make are no different in type from the above, except that often the groups are more general, and the links between the groups and the behaviour more obscure. We expect that people will behave in such a way in a café so that food is provided for us, and we don't need to think about it. We don't necessarily expect that male, protestant divorcees will be more likely to commit suicide than others—as Durkheim showed—and it needs a considerable amount of explanation to indicate why this should be so. The main point is that the *therefore* in the argument above is a logical error. There is no incompatibility between a thing being unique and sharing characteristics with others. Compare two objects. Object *A* has characteristics *p*, *q*, and *r*. Object *B* has characteristics *p*, *q*, and *s*. They are alike, in that they share characteristics *p* and *q*. But they differ from each other in that they do not share characteristics *r* or *s*. Human beings have an almost unlimited number of characteristics, and we are able to analyse them sociologically because everyone shares some characteristics with others, as well as having some different ones, which they probably share with someone else. It is the *total* combination which is unique, not every individual characteristic. Thus, in rational terms, human individuality, uniqueness is no barrier to sociological explanation. Since an individual does not respond to a situation in terms of discrete characteristics, but as a whole person, it is clear that the actual prediction of an individual's behaviour in a situation is a much more difficult job than making general predictions about the likelihood of behaviour occurring in certain groups under certain conditions.

The other kind of argument goes, 'The deterministic type of explanations that sociologists (and psychologists) use are a denial of free will, and thus degrade man.' This is a more difficult argument because it touches on an old controversy of philosophy—free will versus determinism, and also has direct moral overtones. Such an argument should not bedevil sociology. The fact that there are usually cooks in restaurants does not mean that there is any theoretical impossibility that any given cook might decide not to turn up, and that this might be an exercise of his free will. It is true, however, that any social scientist will search for the causes of any behaviour in a person's social experience (in as far as the behaviour isn't innate). But, as we have tried to point out in the first chapter, once we are aware of forces pressuring us to behave in certain ways, then a choice as to whether to continue to so behave or not becomes meaningful. If we are not aware of the reasons for our behaviour, such a choice is not really a choice at all.

On the other hand, it is justifiable to express irritation at the mechanistic way some sociologists, and some schools of sociology approach the study of man, so that instead of an interaction between man and society—a dialectical relationship—there is a one-way adaptation of man to society, an adaptation buttressed by the use of jargon—such as role, norm and deviant—which we shall discuss further below (Pečuljić, 1965, Wrong, 1964). Some sociologists have been led towards this one way approach by the study of undeveloped societies, in which every individual seemed to fit in, and very little behaviour was unexpected, or could not be explained in terms of the groups in the society to which the individual belonged and the way they were related and organized. For others there lies somewhere at the back of the theories an attempt to justify the 'system', to explain it in terms that will dissuade people who suffer in it in various ways from arising in justified wrath to overthrow it. These arguments are part of our constant attack on that approach to sociology which can be labelled functionalist, and which, in its pervasive varieties and influence, we are seeking to combat throughout this book. Such approaches need criticism, but although to do so in terms of an argument about free will is an understandable mistake, it lets the culprit off the hook too easily.

Public issues and personal troubles

So far, we have tried to show that the usual objections to sociological types of explanation are not well founded, but that there are sociological reasons, deriving from the prior socialization of the students, why many students hold rather strongly to these objections. We have also taken the opportunity to attack the mechanistic approach to sociology which explains human behaviour in terms of a one way adaptation of man to society. However, it is vital to recognize the pervasiveness of the social, and the importance of sociological explanation in understanding human behaviour and social problems. In our view this involves cultivating a way of looking at social problems, and of trying to explain behaviour, a specific kind of sensitivity. C. Wright Mills, with whose general approach to sociology we are in considerable agreement, has called this the 'sociological imagination', while Peter Berger in *Invitation to Sociology*, expresses the same idea in cruder form (Mills, 1959a, Berger, 1963, ch. 2). Mills argues that in the complex modern world of great states and constant change, it is above all this 'imagination' that helps us to ask the right sort of questions so that we can begin to explain the social problems that face us. If one man is unemployed, he says, that is a personal problem for that man, a trouble. As long as there are jobs available, we look to his character or training for an explanation. But when a large proportion (how large?) of a nation's labour force is unemployed, it is impossible to explain this in terms of individuals—we must look to the groups they belong to and their organization, the way society is organized, for an explanation. It becomes an *issue*. Another example Mills gives is of marriage—if one marriage breaks down, this is a personal problem. When, as in contemporary America, one quarter of all marriages end in divorce (50 per cent in the Los Angeles area), then, although it appears as a personal problem to each couple, we are justified in seeking an explanation outside the individual couple, in terms of their group memberships and their organization—in the way society is organized. Stokely Carmichael makes the same point in another way, substituting the terms individual and institutionalized for troubles and issues:

> When unidentified white terrorists bomb a black church and kill five black children, that is an act of individual racism, widely deplored by most segments of the world. But when in that same city, Birmingham, Alabama, five hundred black babies die each year because of lack of proper food, shelter and medical facilities, and thousands more are destroyed or maimed physically, emotionally and intellectually because of conditions of poverty and discrimination in the black community, that is a function of institutionalised racism (Carmichael, 1968).

If *troubles* are defined as being largely personal in origin, and *issues* as largely social in origin, Mills argues that, because we experience all events in a personal way, we tend to underestimate the explanation in terms of issues. It is necessary therefore to establish the importance and widespread relevance of the sociological type of explanation, and we shall try to do this by considering two areas of study, one of which is often considered to depend largely upon biology, and the other, one of the most personal, individual kinds of problem, in order to show how important it is to be aware of sociological explanations.

Examples of the pervasiveness of social influences

1 Men and women

Who asks whom to dance? Who usually takes most part in bringing up the children in a marriage? Who does more of the cooking? of the housework? Who is more likely to stop work on marriage? and even more likely to stop on having children? Who generally makes sexual advances? Who spends more time on personal adornment? Who is evaluated by others at least as much in terms of their personal attractiveness as in terms of the work they do or other qualities? Almost everyone will have no difficulty in answering these questions, and a majority, though by no means all, will also be describing their own behaviour in giving the answer they consider appropriate. What is the reason for the different ways of behaving that most people expect of men and women in our society today? Because there are physiological and biological differences between men and women, it is very often assumed that physiology and biology are directly responsible for these different ways of behaviour. For men and women to behave as they usually do is not a social, but a natural thing, runs the argument. From this it is easy to characterize people who don't behave in the expected ways as somehow unnatural. Margaret Mead, in a famous book, *Sex and Temperament in Three Primitive Societies*, set out to show, by using examples from her studies in New Guinea, that many of the differences between the sexes often attributed to biology are, in fact, social in origin (Mead, 1935). One of the advantages of New Guinea as an area of investigation is that, although there are many different societies there, there has been historically relatively little mixing among them for long periods, so that, within a relatively small geographical area, many different ways of doing things can be found. The Arapesh tribe, Mead points out, made very little distinction between the ways of behaving of the different sexes. Assertiveness or aggressiveness, which, in our society, are usually attributed to men, are not characteristic of the behaviour of either sex among the Arapesh, among whom there is an uniform lack of ambition. Even the biological fact that women have to have the children is socially minimized. Men lie down with their wives immediately after childbirth, and, by some process of self-suggestion that seems to work for both man and woman, men 'take over' much of the fatigue, lessening the suffering of the woman. We find, however, that in as far as heavy carrying work is done in this primitive society, it is performed by the women, who are supposed to be equipped 'naturally' with specially strong foreheads for the purpose. Mead explains the lack of aggressiveness by reference to the practice of late weaning of children, and the fact that any child will be fed by any mother who can give milk. She compares the Arapesh to the *Mundugamor*, a tribe of recently 'pacified' head hunters living some distance away. Here aggressiveness was a characteristic of both men and women in equal measure. She describes love-making as a battle between the partners, from which each returns bruised and torn. It is explained that children are reared with extreme disregard, many first born being drowned, with adults showing little affection for children. More basically, however, we would propose that both the characteristics, and the childrearing practices of the Arapesh and the Mundugamor derived from the ways they had of procuring their food, which, since they were at subsistence level, was a constant preoccupation. The Arapesh obtained it by cultivating the land; the Mundugamor, historically, to a considerable extent by killing people from other neighbouring societies. Aggressiveness is not connected with the former, but very relevant to the latter. In a third tribe, the Tchambuli, some of the attributes often ascribed to men and women in our society seemed actually to be reversed. Men adorned themselves, and gossiped, and were selected by the women, who made sexual advances, did all the trade upon which the society depended, although the men made many of the traded items. Women were dominant and aggressive, and female homosexuality was common. Mead points to the fact that girls were brought up smoothly within a circle of women, but that boys were thrown out at an early age, and for a period seemed spurned by all, thus becoming insecure, and constantly seeking affection. But, more basically, it appears that this society used to be one in which head hunting went on, but that this, for some unspecified reason, became less important, perhaps because of the high value that other groups placed upon the mosquito nets that the Tchambuli learned how to produce. Since the men had been specialized as head hunters, the division of labour in the society had changed, leaving the men with no clear position. It is also interesting to notice that in Tchambuli, the natural and created resources were sufficient to enable attention to be diverted from food gathering so that art could develop.

Here, therefore, we have three societies in which the expectations about how men and women should behave differed widely from those often found in Britain today, and from each other. But how can we tell which behaviour is more natural? No doubt, members of each of the societies would describe their behaviour as natural. By comparing each with the other, and all with our own society, we are driven to the conclusion that the problem is not biological, but social, and that the sources of the behaviour and attitudes of men and women are to be sought not in their physiological make up, but in the ways their societies are arranged. Margaret Mead compares several societies. She uses the comparative method. This is very helpful for the sort of problem which proposes that certain forms of behaviour are universal, or natural. By the investigation of the variety of behaviour in different societies we can test whether such statements are true or not. History can be used in the same way, to test the validity of propositions about the universality or naturalness of patterns of behaviour. Perhaps in our own society in previous times, things were done differently, in which case we can ascribe a social derivation to the particular phenomenon under study.

Another important thing can be noticed about the description of the three societies we have given above. Mead gives particular emphasis to patterns of bringing up children in accounting for the differences in the societies. The explanation is in terms of socialization. But we have tried to suggest that the method in which a society's wealth (in these cases, food) is produced, and, with the Tchambuli, the change in the basis of production, lie behind both the behaviour, and the socialization. From the evidence given, such an explanation seems eminently reasonable. But it does illustrate how the things that different sociologists consider important can affect not only their explanation of *what* they observe, but also what they consider is worth emphasizing in what they observe, which brings us back to the problems of sociologists we talked of in the first chapter.

We have tried to show that something commonly assumed to be biological in origin is, in fact, social, in order to illustrate the pervasiveness of the social, the importance of sociological explanation, which is the main theme of this section. We can also notice that sociological investigation is relevant to the problems about the relationships of women to homes and childbearing, problems which are frequently written about as 'women's problems' in the 'quality' press, since more middle class women have begun to demand the right to work, and there has been more economic pressure for them to work. It is often argued that it is unnatural and wrong for a woman to work while she has young children, and many women have considerable conflicts over the cross pressures they feel themselves subject to. Of course, working class women historically have never had the opportunity of such a choice. By and large, where work has been available for them, they have had to take it, out of economic necessity. As working class people have struggled to improve their standards of living, the same kind of choice, and dilemma, begins to become meaningful for some of them. But a glance at today's world shows us that expectations about women's relationships to family and work are not the same everywhere, but vary from society to society, and are also changing within the same societies. These 'women's problems' derive from the structure of the society, rather than from the women themselves. An interesting United Nations study illustrates this. This study compared psychiatrists' reports of the causes of neurosis in married women with families, in different countries (World Health Organization, 1966). A psychiatrist from Czechoslovakia reported that problems were very frequent among that group of women who were not working, but spent their time at home with their children. Those who combined work with the upbringing of children were less likely to suffer neuroses. On the other hand, a psychiatrist from Spain, reporting on problems of middle class and wealthier Spanish women, reported the opposite. It was those who *did* combine work and child upbringing who had mental strain. How can we reconcile these contradictory reports? The problem is solved once we know that in Czechoslovakia, it is normal for women with young children to do a job, and that in Spain it is not normal for middle class and wealthier women with young children to do a job. It becomes clear that the causes of the problems of the women are social in nature—the problem is that their behaviour is in conflict with the expectations of most of the people with whom they associate, and this gives rise to tensions which are expressed as neuroses. We might also point out that arguments about women's 'biological' specialization as child upbringer, etc., have been utilized to preserve the social, economic and sexual subordination of women (Mitchell, 1966).

2 Suicide

In our demonstration of the pervasiveness of the social, we have taken an example of relationships widely thought to be biological or 'natural' in origin, and shown that they can only be explained when we know something of the social context in which they occur. Let us take another kind of example to strengthen the point. For most people, the act of *suicide* will seem the most individual of acts, a decision taken by an individual at the utmost extremity of personal despair or depression. And yet it was this problem which was made the subject of one of the most famous of the sociological studies at the turn of the twentieth century, *Suicide*, by Emile Durkheim (1952). One of the reasons why Durkheim himself undertook this study was to try to show that the study of behaviour was not reducible totally to the study of individuals. He wrote in his preface to the book:

> It is not realized that there can be no sociology unless societies exist, and that societies cannot exist if there are only individuals (p. 38).

It was this attack against reducing sociology to psychology that sometimes led Durkheim to overstress his point and give the impression of agelicism which we have discussed in the first chapter. Durkheim made no attempt at all to approach individuals who had attempted suicide, to ask for their reasons. Nor did he seek the co-operation of relatives of known suicides. What he did was to collect together the statistics on the number of suicides for various European countries during the nineteenth century, and to analyse them. A most striking fact emerged. If suicide was an act of individual despair, into which no social components entered, it would be reasonable to expect fairly wide variations in suicide rates in any society from year to year. Yet, in spite of the small number of cases compared to the total populations, the suicide *rates* from year to year were remarkably steady, steadier, in fact, than the birth and death rates for particular societies. Durkheim considered carefully all the explanations for suicides that had been put forward up to that time, based on such factors as climate, race, mental illness, heredity, and contagion (the idea that one suicide sparks off others). In a section of his book that is an absolute tour de force of sociology, he showed that all these explanations were untenable, either because they were logically flawed, or because propositions which they entailed could be shown to be untrue when compared with the available statistics. It did become clear, however, that the incidence of suicide was more frequent at some times of the day than others, and at some seasons of the year than others, namely, that it was more frequent in summer than in winter, and more frequent in mid-morning and afternoon than at any other time. Durkheim also found numerous other correlations. We should not think that he discovered them by chance, and then built a theory to account for them, although this is the impression given by the lay out of the book; nor that Durkheim had a ready made theory which enabled him to look for all the 'right' facts. We can assume that his general orientation to sociology, in combination with the material of previous research, in combination with the results of the researches he carried out, all these, in what we might call a dialectical interaction, led him to the propositions which he finally presented in his book as if they were a logical progression from the particular to the general. It is important to point this out, because the fallacy that theories and models are derived from the accumulation of small pieces of evidence is still quite common in sociology, as is an alternative view that one has to build a whole theory *first*, and then test it afterwards (see Chapter 6). Durkheim discovered that the likelihood of suicide was related to the religion that a person belonged to. Protestants were more likely to commit suicide than Catholics, and Jews were least prone of all. Suicide was also related to the type of family life people led. Married people with children were less likely to commit suicide than unmarried people or widows and widowers. For women who were, or had been married, those who did not have children committed suicide more frequently. He also noticed that suicide rates were reduced at times when important political events which involved people were occurring, such as crucial elections, popular wars, etc., Durkheim was able to see a common link in all these relationships. It was the degree of integration of the individual into the society. Protestant religious beliefs, with their emphasis on the direct relationship between an individual and God (or their conscience), do not provide such a complete framework of integration as the Catholic, while Jewish religious beliefs and institutions are the most integrative of all. The unmarried, widowed, are not as well integrated into a family unit, while the fact that suicide is reduced when there is greater political activity of a popular nature suggests that political integration is also related to suicide. Durkheim put forward three propositions. The likelihood of suicide will vary, he said, inversely with the degree of religious, family and political integration. The more an individual is integrated into one or all of these spheres, the less the likelihood of suicide. From this he proposed a type of suicide which he calls egoistic, caused by lack of social integration. The explanation of why suicide occurs more frequently in the summer and in late morning and afternoon also follows logically from this proposition, because it is at these seasons and times that there is most interaction among people in European societies, so a person who is not integrated feels it most at these times.

Durkheim also noticed two other, general features. Firstly, suicide was much more common in towns, and secondly, suicide rates had tended to increase over the century. Durkheim argued that life in towns was more impersonal, 'anomic' than life in the country, and that the process of industrialization in the nineteenth century was increasing the importance of the towns. It appeared that to some extent, the framework for integration was itself breaking down, so that it was becoming less easy for individuals to be integrated. Durkheim was very concerned with this trend, which he considered indicated a degree of social illness, social pathology, and he suggested that there was a second type of suicide, anomic, deriving from situations where the individual had no stable framework into which to integrate.

Finally, Durkheim noticed that people also killed themselves in situations where there was a very high degree of integration of the individual into the social group, as in primitive or traditional societies, and in the officer corps in the armed services. He concluded from this that, in some social situations, the individual could be so highly integrated into society that he valued his own life less than the acceptance of the social demands made on him, so that either for honour, or for shame at some transgression of these social demands, he would sacrifice his life so that demands could be maintained or reinforced. This led Durkheim to posit a third category of suicide, which he named altruistic.

Subsequent research has modified but not invalidated Durkheim's statistical findings, but the particular detail of this or that proposition is not what concerns us here (Giddens, 1965, 1966). What Durkheim has succeeded in demonstrating is that the individual act of suicide, isolated and infrequent though it is, cannot be explained without the consideration of the social relationships which all individuals in various ways depend upon. It should be noted that this kind of approach does not enable us to predict which individual will commit suicide, but only to predict those social groups from which suicides will most frequently come, and why. It is also not possible to accept Durkheim's proposition that there was a sort of social pathology involved in increasing suicide rates, since, even if suicide is regarded as a social evil, other social goods might be increasing at the same time, thus cancelling out the bad effect overall. Furthermore, different social groups, in different positions in social structures, have different ideas as to what is socially desirable or undesirable, as do the same groups in different historical circumstances, so that an agreed social pathology is unlikely—aspects of this argument will be developed further in the next chapter. We have used Durkheim's work to illustrate one simple, but very important, indeed crucial argument; the pervasiveness of the social. The two examples we have chosen from very diverse fields are meant to drive this point home.

Roles ✓

At the beginning of the chapter, when attacking the argument against sociology in terms of free will, we indicated our dissatisfaction with the sort of sociology that relates societies and people in terms of the adjustment of the latter to the former. These approaches to sociology all derive from functionalism, which will be criticized later. If there is any one idea which is responsible for the grosser crudities of the 'one-way adjustment' approach, it is that of *role*, and, since a lot of sociology students are sure to be told that the idea of role is the key to the understanding of the relationship between society and person, it is certainly worth while giving some consideration to it here, so as not to let such sociologists have it all their own way.

One general difficulty is the vague way in which the term is so often used in sociological work. The first thing, when you find 'role' being extensively used, is to notice how it is defined by the particular writer, or whether, as is often the case, the reader is left to attach to the term whatever meaning he wishes. One can ask: does role denote a social position—shop steward, surgeon, student? Does it describe how a person in such a position actually behaves, 'performs his part'? Does it describe how other people expect a surgeon or shop steward to behave? If the latter, which people's expectations prescribe the role? In the case of a shop steward, will it be the expectations of the management, or of his fellow workers, or of trade union officials? Why one rather than another? Does role refer to a position in a particular situation—the surgeon in the operating theatre—or does the 'role' follow the incumbent of the position around? Does society have 'needs' which men fulfil by playing roles? Arising out of all this, what view of man and society are implicit in role theory?

The term role comes from acting, of course. An actor playing a role in the theatre is performing for others a part whose outline has been drawn, not by himself, but by the author of the play. The actor is deliberately not himself, but someone else. Because society, the social, is so pervasive, as we have tried to show, sociologists have often been tempted to argue that all of us are in fact playing parts, not laid down by an author, but by 'society' —an idea we have already criticized. The appeal of this analogy may partly lie in the fact that sociologists are members of groups (middle class, upwardly mobile, academic) among whom the playing of parts, more or less deliberately, forms a considerable amount of social life, and the success with which one plays these parts, the impres-

sions one creates, are ways of gaining status and recognition from one's fellows (c.f. the popularity of Stephen
Potter's works on 'lifemanship', 'oneupmanship', etc.).
Since the idea gets a boost from the sociologist's social
background, it is tempting for him to go on and develop it.
The whole of social life may be interpreted as role playing; everyone is acting all the time. And some sociologists
hold this position. Professor Banton, in his book, *Roles*
(1965), which is, in effect, an introduction to sociology,
argues that almost all human behaviour and almost all
the ideas of sociology can be interpreted in terms of 'role
theory'.

The fundamental difficulty with such a view is that it
assumes that there is, or ought to be, agreement about how
people in particular positions should behave:

> For the time being it is necessary to assume in the
> examination of particular roles that there is agreement
> among all the parties affected as to the definition of
> the role in question (Banton, 1965, p. 36).

> People expect appropriate behaviour from the holder of
> a particular position. The sum of these expectations is
> the role (Frankenberg, 1966, p. 16-17).

The reader is referred also to the example from Berger
(1963) discussed on p. 17. It is important to ask whether
it is valid to start with such assumptions, and whether
we can add together the expectations of different people
and thus find what a particular role is. Let us do so by
taking an example—the social position of the school-
teacher.

Teachers exist in many societies, and have existed over
many centuries; within this country at the present time
they may be employed by local authorities or by private
bodies; they may be women or men; their pupils may be
five year olds or eighteen year olds, and come from any
social background; they may teach in a large city or a
remote rural area. Before we could talk about the 'teacher's

39

role' in general we should have to establish that there were
common elements everywhere and at all times which
go beyond the general definition of teacher. However,
even if we decide on the exact structural location of the
teacher in a particular type of school, we must also take
into account all the different groups of people who have
some interest in what she does. These would include the
other teachers in the school, the pupils, the headteacher,
the parents, the H.M.I.s, the local authority advisers, and
administrators, education college tutors, and so on. How
do these people think the teacher should behave? How
far can we assume that they will agree? Studies by Gross
(1958) in the U.S., and by Musgrove and Taylor (1969) in
Britain, indicate that, while such different groups may
have particular expectations of school superintendants or
school teachers, there may not be agreement between the
groups as to what is expected. In an attempt to avoid
the undercutting of the whole concept of role which
these disagreements imply, the idea of role conflict is
generally introduced to describe situations where there are
conflicting expectations of the holder of a particular
position. Merton (1957) has played down the significance
of these conflicts, because some of the groups of people
involved are not very powerful, or do not actually see
what the teacher does. Power relationships are not static,
however, and expectations of those who cannot directly
observe the teacher may nonetheless be important.

Although these, and endless other elaborations of 'role
theory' have to acknowledge the existence of conflicting
expectations, the assumption that consensus somehow
ought to exist is not discarded; if it were, the whole basis
of role theory would collapse. Thus, while we see that
people's notions of how those in particular social positions
(teacher, waitress, students, etc.) should behave vary
according to their own group membership, and while we
have already discussed the way in which individuals may

be influenced by the expectations which others have of them, we are suggesting that, because of its faulty assumptions, 'role theory' is unable to further our understanding of these expectations, their influence and effect.

If, instead of talking about roles, we talk about the expectations held by specified groups as to the behaviour of people in certain positions, it makes it much easier to check the correctness and consequences of these expectations, and leads us away from the sort of mechanical idea of sociology that society 'creates', via social organization, sets of roles to which a person 'has to' conform, an idea which underlies the thinking of many sociologists. Definition in terms of expectations gives us a much more flexible, dynamic model, in which a person's behaviour in a position depends on an interaction between his own learned expectations and the pressures put upon him by others with possibly different expectations, and which also depends on the power they have over him, an interaction which will be in constant change as the power relationships change—in other words, a dialectical relationship. Reverting to the example of the school teacher, the approach used by Webb in his article, *The Sociology of a School*, in which he examines the varying types of pressures which will face a teacher in a slum secondary modern school, offers a potentially more adaptable and dynamic perspective than can be found in most writing on the 'teacher's role' in the sociology of education texts (Webb, 1962).

In general, the theorizing about roles appears to us to be one of the most arid areas of sociological endeavour; starting from inadequate ideas and building up mountains of qualifications and sub-qualifications, it is an occupation which can keep an agile brain busy for years and even secure career advancement, but which tells us virtually nothing at all about the world we live in (e.g. Biddle and Thomas, 1966). The danger of confusing the analogy with what it is supposed to illuminate (a danger which we shall examine further in the next chapter) can be illustrated here, too. When Goffman views social life as a play, with men as role-takers, actors, performers (only one of the analogies he develops), he tends to slip into ✓ the sort of mistakes we have outlined above (agelicism), even though his sensitive and acute observations of human behaviour are directed in the main towards a dialectical exploration of the interactions of individuals with the situations in which they find themselves, whether as patients in mental hospitals, surgeons in the operating theatre, or islanders in the Shetlands (Goffman, 1959, 1968, 1969).

3

Social structure

Understanding social structure

Up to now, apart from the development of the idea of the pervasiveness of the social, our approach has tended to be negative—a series of warnings against uncritical acceptance of what is taught as sociology—in the course of which some sociological ideas and ways of analysing problems have been introduced. What positive alternative are we putting up to the approaches we have criticized, at this time the prevailing orthodoxy in the United States, and to some extent in Britain? A considerable number of sociologists pay lip service to the idea of social structure. In our view, providing it is linked with the ideas of social conflict and social change, the idea of social structure is *the* lead off point, and the anchorage idea of sociology. It isn't, however, a completely easy idea to grasp operationally, that is, in use, nor is there agreement among sociologists as to how it should be used or indeed whether it is the central idea at all. In developing your own views on the subject it will be necessary to compare our arguments with those of others.

The idea of social structure is as difficult to define in a few words as is sociology itself (but see Bottomore, 1963, ch. 7). We think of it as a guide which tells us where to look in trying to explain any social phenomenon sociologically, that is, that the explanation of the social phenomenon, or part, or individual in a society should be sought first in the way that society is organized as a whole, in its principles of organization. If you like, social structure is a signpost to the right questions to ask.

All this is very abstract; in order to clarify it, and to develop the idea, we are going to use a simple analogy, and later give some examples from anthropological studies. One analogy, which a large number of sociologists have used in the past in order to try to indicate the way they think that social phenomena ought to be explained, is called the 'organic analogy', and it compares societies to human bodies, organisms (Spenser, 1893, part 2, Radcliffe-Brown, 1963, ch. 9). We do not like this analogy, because it is easy to become so involved in it that one begins to forget that it is an analogy at all, and to come to believe that societies really *are* like organisms. We use instead the analogy of a watch, both positively, to suggest why structure is important, and negatively, to show how plausible are some of the mistakes we consider noted sociologists to have made.

The watch analogy

The most important point to start with is: a watch is more than the sum of its parts. If you have a watch handy as you read this, take it to pieces. Collect all the parts together and put them in your hand. You do not have a watch, but a heap of parts. Therefore, a watch is not just the sum of its parts, but the sum of its parts *plus* the way they are put together, related to each other, organized. In the same way, society is more than the sum of the people in it. It is not only the people, but also the way they are related to each other, organized—the social structure. If this is correct, what goes on in society can't be explained solely in terms of individuals, but only by understanding the way they are related to each other.

The analogy may be developed. A watch can be subdivided into groups of parts—for instance, those connected with the power supply; with regulation; with information; with protection. Within larger groups of parts are smaller groups, till one gets back to the individual part. Some sociologists, using the organic analogy, have tried to say that societies have regulative systems, digestive systems, etc., in the same way as a body has. This use of the analogy is completely misleading. We are *not* trying to say that any particular group of parts in a watch, those connected with information, say (hands, dial, etc.), has an equivalent in society. We are arguing that, as the action of each part is explained by the organization of its group of parts, and the action of its group by the organization of the whole, the structure, so, in society, we can partly explain the action of each individual by the organization of the groups to which he belongs, and the action of the groups partly by the organization of the whole society, the social structure. Notice the modifications to the analogy here. Firstly, to claim a total explanation in terms of structure would be an extreme example of the crude determinism which we have attacked earlier, as well as sociological imperialism—denying to other social sciences, especially psychology, the right to a bit of explanation. Secondly, the same individual, unlike a watch part, belongs to various different groups, so things cannot be so neat as in a watch. But if we think simply of the relation between the parts of a watch and the whole, and suggest that it can be subdivided in terms of subsidiary groups of parts, so we can think of the relation between an individual and social structure, and subdivide it in terms of subsidiary concepts, such as those of institutions and groups. A very simplified little diagram shows what we mean.

SOCIAL STRUCTURE

Initial stage in explaining individual behaviour sociologically:

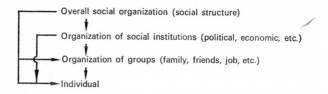

Explore the relationships suggested by the arrows, but please note that the diagram is at this stage static and one-way and thus requires considerable modification.

Let's play with the analogy with a watch a little further. The parts and groups of parts in a watch have a closely defined action in the structure of a watch. The watch is designed for a specific purpose—to tell the time. There can be very little variation in the action of the parts of our watch, since, if they don't do exactly what they are made to do, they are faulty, and we say that the watch is wrong. Perhaps the part is faulty—badly made. Alternatively, the design of the watch may be faulty, so that it puts excessive strain on one group of parts. At this point we think the watch analogy becomes very misleading.

Unlike a watch, there is no external creator of society, nor is there any externally defined purpose for it. Societies are created by the parts (people) of the structure themselves interacting. Since there is no external creator, and no external purpose, it is quite possible that the views of groups of people within the structure may conflict with regard to what purposes the society has, or should have, without our being able to say that there is something wrong either with the people or with the 'design'. Also, although it is theoretically as possible to design societies as it is watches, and several people have put forward blueprints as to how they think society ought to be designed (Auguste Comte, who gave sociology its name, was a dab hand at this—see Mill, 1866), generally speaking, no-one designed the societies that man has lived in up to now. Like Topsy, they just growed. We have to find out how, and why.

Unlike watch parts, therefore, designed for a purpose, persons, groups and institutions may not 'fit in'. Unlike in a watch, conflicts of interest between persons and groups may be part of a social structure in a way they never could be in a watch. Indeed, as we shall argue in the next chapter, one of the main ways of understanding how societies change may be by examining the conflicts of interests between different groups, deriving from their different positions in a social structure, and the differential benefits they receive from these positions.

Varieties of functionalism

We have argued that societies, unlike watches, have no external purpose. But a large number of sociologists disagree with this. They attempt to explain society teleologically (by attributing a purpose to it). Particularly those sociologists who studied primitive societies observed that in many cases, things there really did seem to be a little analogous to a watch—people and groups seemed to fit together rather like the parts of a watch. In order to make sense of what they saw, they developed the following sorts of explanation, which also underlie the way many sociologists today look at societies. Some argued that the purpose of society was the maintenance of social order, and social stability, and that the function of the parts of a society and the way they were organized, the social structure, was to maintain this order and stability. Radcliffe-Brown, a famous British anthropologist, expounded this view. (Radcliffe-Brown, 1963). It is still very influential, and we can call it *structural functionalism*. Another argument was that the purpose of society is the satisfaction of certain biological needs of human beings (Malinowski, 1944, p. 145f.). This can be characterized as *biological functionalism*, and it is not so popular, or so widely used in contemporary sociology as the former (Gluckman, 1944). A third view is a more sophisticated development of the first, based on the idea that the maintenance of order, or equilibrium (another analogy, borrowed from mechanics), is largely achieved by the existence of common values, or norms, shared by the vast majority of the people in the society. The emphasis on norms, rather than on structure, leads this view, popular in the United States and among a number of sociologists in Britain, to be called *normative functionalism*. Its central theorist is Talcott Parsons (Parsons, 1964, Black, 1961, Giddens, 1968, Lessnoff, 1968, Foss, 1963—the last four references are critiques). If the central purpose, the maintenance of order, is accepted, then it is possible to carry the watch analogy further, for instance, to suggest that some parts of a society may be ill, or pathological, which sounds better, because they don't fit in. An example of this idea has already been given in Durkheim's contention that the suicide rate increase in nineteenth-century Europe represented pathological development in the societies in the period. Another famous example is that of Elton Mayo, an American management sociologist, who argued that shop stewards in industry who were seen as non-co-operative by management were in some way ill (Mayo, 1957). The basic fault with all these views is that it is a complete mistake to attribute any sort of purpose at all to society, which, as we have argued above, is not a *thing* like a watch at all, but simply a collective term for a nation of people, their possessions, organization and behaviour. Only people can have purposes, and groups of people in common situations may have common purposes. What these may be, and how they are related to the organization of the society is a matter for investigation, and cannot be decided in advance on theoretical grounds. In spite of this basic mistake, functionalism has been very popular, for two main sorts of reasons. Firstly, it does provide a way of giving order to the tremendous complexity of the whole that is a society, and of by-passing what people *say* are the reasons for their actions, by establishing an alternative basis of explanation for them—we shall see the advantages of this in the examples which follow. Secondly, it is very attractive to those groups in a social structure in whose interests it is to maintain things as they are, as it provides a sophisticated ideology which justifies the status quo. Hence, there has always been a conservative element in functionalist sociology (c.f. Nisbet, 1967). In case it is thought that this kind of view is simply confined to the sphere of sociology, it might be pointed out that the same sort of approach underlies the statements of people who say, for instance, that beatniks are indicators of social decline, or that strikers are 'harming the national interest'. Unlike a watch, harmony among the parts of a society is not an essential part of the structure, so that it is almost impossible to get total agreement as to what the 'national interest' is. As we showed in the first chapter, what one group of people may consider to be in the 'national interest' may not be accepted as such by another group.

Those sociologists, among whom we count ourselves, who reject functionalism in all its forms as a means of understanding society, argue that because society is *not* like a watch, or a body, in the crucial ways examined above, it is necessary to analyse the interests and purposes of groups of people in a society, and see how they are interrelated—in other words, to study the social structure without attributing to societies the characteristics of a person. Because almost all such studies show that actual social structures have developed in such a way that the structure benefits some groups at the expense of others, a potential conflict exists between groups in the social structure, deriving from the structure itself. Sociologists who adopt this method of analysis of societies, which derives from Marx, are often called *structural conflict* theorists, although we would prefer the terms *historical* or *dynamic structuralism* (Lefebvre, 1968).

The watch analogy has enabled us to make several points about the importance of structure as a means of explanation in sociology, about explaining the part in terms of the organization of the whole, and to differentiate between those sociologists who attribute some purpose to the whole, which provides a *function* for each of the parts, and those who do not. This basic difference in orientation leads to several other differences in emphasis, one of which has already been introduced in the discussion of role, and others of which will be discussed later. A further point, of particular importance, must be introduced here. *If our reference point for analysis of societies is some existing purpose, which is always there, the history of how things came to be that way is separate from the explanation of them, and ceases to be of central interest.* To talk about the social structure is to describe how the organization of society 'maintains' order. *On the other hand, if there is no external reference point, the only way we can understand the relationships of groups is by examining how they interact over time—in their historical practice.* By examining this—how some groups benefit and others react, for instance—we can ascertain the principles by which the society is organized, its social structure, and from this, the pressures for change and the resistances to it. In functionalist sociology, therefore, the study of history and change is at a discount—as can be seen from the contents' list of Broom and Selznick's book given in the first chapter. In structural conflict sociology, it is essential—see the contents list of Fiamengo's book. Discussion of this point is continued in Chapters 4 and 6.

Culture

A large number of American sociologists assign the concept of structure a subordinate place to that of culture in their approach (e.g., Benedict, 1952, Linton, 1961). The argument may be expressed in its simplest form like this. Most psychologists and sociologists are now agreed that instinct is of little significance in the explanation of human behaviour, which overwhelmingly derives from what we learn. What we learn derives from our culture—the sets of established ways of doing things developed in a society. Each individual as he grows up is socialized (trained) to internalize (accept as his own) this culture. Therefore, the central concept in explaining behaviour is culture:

Culture→Social Learning→Individual

Most of these sociologists are heavily influenced by Freudian psychology, arguing that the really important learning period is in early childhood. Returning to our analogy for a moment, humans are, in this view, a bit like watch parts—once they are made (in early childhood), they don't change. Once again, these views seem plausible when we study some primitive societies—examples have been given of Margaret Mead's studies of sex and temperament, where she explains different behaviour and attitudes in men and women in terms of different child upbringing in the different societies. But this approach gives no explanation—other than historical accident—of why cultures differ, both between societies, and—most importantly when studying our own societies—among different groups of people within societies (Worsley, 1957a). We would argue that the key to this problem lies in an understanding of how the way a society is organized has developed, placing structure before culture:

Social Structure→Culture→Social Learning→individual. This is why, in our use of Mead's work in the second chapter, we have reinterpreted her explanations. Furthermore, while acknowledging the importance of the early years of life in explaining behaviour, we would want to emphasize that, in any complex society, many differing and often potentially conflicting ideas are learned by the young, and that we need an approach which acknowledges the importance of later socialization in explaining behaviour (c.f. Orlansky, 1949, Lindesmith and Strauss, 1950).

Analytic and descriptive uses

We have attempted to introduce the idea of structure analytically, i.e., as a means of understanding the principles underlying the inter-relationship of social groups in a society, and how these interrelationships developed and are developing. This is the usage adopted by Marx and by Levy-Strauss, the famous French anthropologist (Godelier, 1967). There is another way of using the idea of structure, so that it is much more *descriptive*, a sort of catalogue of the institutions of a society. This is the approach adopted by Nadel, who distinguishes it clearly from Levy-Strauss':

> For Levy-Strauss and Leach, structure is an explanatory construct meant to provide the key to the observed facts of social existence ... I consider social structure, ... to be still the social reality itself, or an aspect of it, not the logic behind it; and I consider structural analysis to be no more than a descriptive method, however sophisticated, not a piece of explanation (Nadel, 1965).

There is obviously no harm in describing the institutions of a society, but unless one has some explanatory principles, it is impossible to know what to single out as worthy of description, and this is why such descriptive uses generally smuggle in *implicit* explanatory principles.

The same distinction is often made when we use the term structure in everyday language. For instance, if we say that a building is a structure, this directs our attention to a description of its features, the number and position of its windows, its type of roofing, its shape, etc. If we say that it has a structure, this directs our attention to the means that the designer has adopted to ensure that it doesn't collapse. (But remember that no one designs societies, and that social structure does not exist to ensure that they don't collapse.) Of course, just as analysis involves description, so the analytic use of the idea of structure in sociology involves the descriptive use, but the former is more important, because it is our purpose to find a means of explaining things.

Structure and behaviour

It may help in trying to understand things sociologically if we give a very simple analytic schema of the way structure can affect behaviour, remembering also the simple diagram we have introduced above, and that the relationships are not simply one way. The way a society is organized might be thought of as affecting an individual's behaviour directly, by compelling a person to do something, or making it impossible for him to do something, or it might affect his behaviour indirectly, so that, while it is not impossible for him to choose an alternative course of action, he is more or less strongly pressured, either towards or away from a source of action. An example will illustrate each condition. In a primitive society with a very restricted division of labour, there is only one path that a person can take in life. In Arapesh society, a man will till the tribe's gardens. In this very simple society, in which the structure lies in the people's mode of production, there is a direct positive influence on a person's behaviour. In our society, action is directly limited by the structure in many respects. For instance, in the area of job choice, investigators have noted that more people wish to get printing apprenticeships than there are jobs available (Pallister, 1938, Veness, 1962). Some *must* therefore be disappointed. On a more general scale, in a society like ours, where the prestige of occupations, as indicated by the various kinds of material rewards given, is of a roughly pyramidal nature—i.e., the better a job, the fewer there are of them —the idea that anybody with sufficient talent can get to the top, though commonly expressed in this country and even more in the United States, is an absolute impossibility, since, however capable the general population is, only a tiny proportion can fill the small number of jobs at the top.

In our complex societies, very diverse patterns of behaviour are theoretically open to every individual. Therefore, the understanding of indirect pressures, working via socialization and culture, varying according to a person's position in the social structure, becomes very important for the explanation of why individuals behave in one way rather than another. We have already discussed this kind of influence in the first chapter, in relation to sociologists themselves. To take another, simple example. How many young people in our society have read the Communist Manifesto? An enquiry in the basic Sociology class of a Scottish university over three years gives a proportion of rather under 3% for this social group. However, almost 100% have read the Bible (at least, parts of it). Without having done any investigation, it is fairly reasonable to suppose that the figures would be roughly reversed in the Soviet Union. Now, it is not prohibited to read the Bible in the Soviet Union, nor the Communist Manifesto in this country. We do not accept that the differences are the result of chance. It is not adequate to say that they just reflect the differing cultures in the two countries, because, in fact, this is only saying that it is due to chance in a more sophisticated way. Although it comes nearer to an explanation, it is not adequate to say that these books serve in some way to maintain the social order, social stability or equilibrium in the different societies, because it assumes that societies have some such order-maintaining purposes built in—the functionalist line of argument which we have already attacked. In order to understand the different importance of the two books in the different societies, we have to analyse the means which dominant groups in the societies, in their historical struggle to achieve and maintain their dominance, have used to try to *legitimize* the social structure that results—a complex problem in the sociology of social consciousness, the general subject of Chapter 5. This approach does not necessarily mean that some smaller or larger group of people sat down and decided this or that. Sometimes groups of people do make such decisions, affecting social events and behaviour, but very often things develop as by-products of decisions or lack of them in other areas of social life, or, most importantly, as a result of processes of interaction between groups in a social structure.

International structures and interactions between structures

We have so far examined the idea of social structure with respect to individual societies. No society remains totally without contact with other societies. To some extent, therefore, its social structure is affected by others. In some primitive societies, this contact does not seem of great importance. But in others the whole social organization is based on it (Malinowski, 1922). Throughout human history, great empires have been a feature of civilization, so that, for instance, to examine the structure of Jewish society at the time of Christ, without examining the dialectic of its relations with the Roman empire and *its* organization

would clearly lead to a very incomplete and faulty understanding.

Today, we are ceaselessly being told about how small
the world is becoming, how nations are interdependent,
etc., yet a very small proportion of sociologists consider
international structural relations in examining social
phenomena. Not only do we have to put up with a history-
less sociology, but with an insular sociology as well. One
of the most glaring examples of this is in the study of the
poor countries of the world—the so-called 'Third World'
—where sociologists from the 'developed' countries usually
totally ignore the historical development of structural relations between the poor and the rich nations (for exceptions to this see Barratt-Brown, 1963, Frank, 1966, 1967a,
and Jalee, 1968, among others). The varieties of possible
relationships between nations are large, and their effects
on different groups within national social structures may
be very different. (See especially Frank, 1967a for examples.) We cannot go further here than to say that any
sociology which does not give international relationships
adequate weight is a pseudo-science, a statement which
becomes more self-evidently true with every day that
passes, for never have interactions between nations developed at such a pace.

Examples from social anthropology

We introduced the idea of social structure with the help of
an analogy; perhaps some examples will help to clarify
the method of structural analysis, and differentiate it from
the functionalist approach. When Gluckman studied the
Zulu people of S.E. Africa, he found that each year there
was a ceremony to celebrate the goddess Nomkubulwana,
who was the goddess of crop fertility (Gluckman, 1955).
During this ceremony, the women took over the jobs, the
behaviour and even the clothes of the men, who remained

in the huts, and were liable to be attacked if they went near the women. What is the explanation for this reversal of normally expected behaviour? If we were to ask a member of the society, we should be told that, by pleasing the goddess, it ensured good harvests. Since to us there would appear to be no good reason why the practice should actually lead to greater fertility, we are led to reject this explanation and to seek another. Following Merton, we could call this explanation, given by the participants themselves, the *manifest* one (Merton, 1964, ch. 1). We are searching for another kind of explanation, however, which may not be recognized by the participants themselves—this is the *latent* explanation. (Since Merton is a functionalist, he talks of the manifest and latent functions of actions. We prefer to think of the manifest and latent explanations of actions.) An ordinary traveller observing the ritual sees it simply as bizarre, perhaps evidence of the 'backwardness of the natives'; a cultural anthropologist sees it as evidence of the rich diversity of human behaviour. A structural functionalist gets much further. His constant question is, 'How does what goes on function to maintain the social order?' This question gives him a way into the problem. On further study, it becomes clear that the women have a pretty hard time of it in several ways in Zulu society. The practice can then be seen to be a ritual 'let out' for the frustrations of the women, a kind of safety valve, so that for one day they can take over, the psychological release obtained making the other 364 days bearable. In this way, the functionalist argues, social order is maintained, and the ritual has a function. We may interpret this example in an alternative way, avoiding the metaphysics involved in attributing to society the purpose of maintaining order, by asking the question, 'In whose interests is the society organized; which social group benefits at the expense of others?' By analysing social practice in the society over time, it becomes clear that the men benefit at the expense of the women, and we are led to the conclusion that the ritual has developed as a way by which the subordination of the women to the men in the society is reinforced, a safety valve, by means of which the tensions arising from the constant potential conflict created by the structural dominance of the men over the women are deflected from possible attempts by the women to change the structure to their advantage, into a yearly ritual. Rituals of a similar character to this (in which a dominant group becomes subordinate for a day, and a subordinate group dominant) are not infrequent. Roman officers served their men once a year, and it is often reputed that in British public schools, fags were served by their superiors on one day. This is one way in which subordinate groups can be induced to accept their subordination, thus making the annual ritual a worthwhile insurance premium for the dominant groups. Once again, there is no suggestion that a group of Zulu men sat down and decided that the women were getting troublesome, so it was necessary to devise a new ritual to keep them quiet. The ritual developed as the structure did, and people in the society more or less genuinely believe that it is a fertility ritual. Only an analysis of the structure gives us a means of 'demystifying' the practice.

Here is another, more detailed example, taken from Oberg's study of the Uganda Ankole (Oberg, 1961). It was first published in 1940, and referred to the structure of the society before the British colonial period. We ought to note straight away that the study is an historical reconstruction, and that the organization and practices described no longer exist. Oberg attempts to add a time dimension to his study, in spite of the fact that there is no written history, by making cautious use of legends and fireside stories told by the Ankole people. Ankole society has certain resemblances to the feudal society of mediaeval Europe, which could equally have been used as an example to illustrate ideas of structure put forward here.

The Ankole live in an area between Lake Victoria and the Ruwenzori mountain mass, an area which is reasonably fertile, capable of providing surplus resources over minimum population needs, even with very simple agricultural methods. Historically, if the legends are to be believed, the Bairu (serfs), peasant agriculturalists, were invaded by a group of pastoralists displaced from the north by wars, a group smaller in numbers, but superior in fighting ability. They were able to conquer the Bairu and to settle in the country. This group was called the Bahima (nobles). The stories also tell of another invasion by a still more militarily capable group, who moved on but left one of their number behind to be king over the land. From him all later kings are descended. Whatever the details, it appears that the Bahima conquered the Bairu, and, over time, a social structure developed in which the dominance of the former was established. Ankole was surrounded by other societies of similar social organization and there were frequent wars or raids between them. A remarkable succession ritual existed in Ankole.

When a king seemed to be becoming infirm, he was given poison by court magicians, and a new king selected in the following way. A powerful Muhima (kingmaker, singular form of Bahima) took the sacred drum (the church)—the symbol of supreme religious and secular authority, the perfect king—and hid it. Then all the king's sons—there were usually many, as the king had the right to any virgin in the kingdom as his wife—with the exception of the favourite son, took what followers they could from the court, and fought battles till all but one had been killed or driven into exile. Only the powerful Bahima in the border regions did not take part in these battles. Then the winner fought it out with the favourite son and his followers, the eventual winner of this fight being awarded the drum and the kingship by the kingmaker. The whole process might take six or eight months. During this time, a state of partial anarchy reigned in the kingdom, with people taking the opportunity of settling old scores by blood revenge. Meanwhile, at the court, the Bairu servants elected a mock 'king' who 'reigned' over the court Bairu until the struggle for the real kingship was over. He was then ceremonially beheaded by the incoming king. Without a theory of social structure, all this appears as bizarre —a grotesque example of primitivism—and was reported as such by early travellers from Europe visiting the region, such as Burton and Speke. A functionalist can do much better. By reference to the universal principle of the maintenance of order which societies 'have', he can show that the practices of the Ankole succession help to keep the existing order going. Although this is much better than nothing, as we have argued, it is based on a false premise— the reification of society into a being that can have purposes. In our view, the key to the explanation of the Ankole practices is via an understanding of the social structure, and the key to this is given by the history, sketchy as it is, which indicates that the social structure favours the Bahima as a social group, in terms of wealth and power. Oberg analysed the relations between the Bahima and the Bairu in detail. The Bairu had to give tribute to the Bahima in grain and labour. They were not allowed to own productive cows, the Bahima's 'status symbol'. No Mwiru (singular form of *Bairu*) could marry a Muhima, nor could a Mwiru become a Muhima in any other way—his position was ascribed (fixed by birth). A Muhima could take blood revenge against a Mwiru who he considered to have wronged him, but a Mwiru had no right of blood revenge against a Muhima. Furthermore, although there were frequent wars, all the fighting was done by the Bahima, because no Mwiru was allowed to possess weapons. Thus the Bairu as a group were in every way subordinate to the Bahima. A potential conflict between the groups is built into the structure, and out of the striving by the Bahima, the dominant group, to stop the potential conflict from becoming real, explanations for the events emerge. Thus, the refusal to allow the Bairu to have arms, which, although it weakened the military potential of the Ankole, was necessary for the Bahima, in case the more numerous Bairu turned them against the Bahima. Now we can begin to understand the part of the succession ritual concerning the mock Mwiru 'king'. In this ritual, we see the social recognition of the potential aspirations of the Bairu to a different social position, and, in the beheading of the 'king', a dramatization of the consequences of such an attempt. This is another way in which the Bairu were kept from trying to change their position, derived from the symbolic aspects of the kingship and the Sacred Drum (served by priests). These were supposed to provide justice, so that any Mwiru could appeal to them if wronged by a Muhima, and could not say that there was not a final human, and even supernatural arbiter of his case. However, Oberg's analysis of the practice of justice by king and Drum reveals that the structural subordination of the Bairu is reflected in it. The saying goes that, 'The Bahima are the cattle of Bagyendanwa (drum) and the Bairu are his goats.' Cattle were superior to goats in Ankole. Furthermore, it was necessary for both parties in a dispute to give king or drum gifts to get justice, and the Bahima had more wealth than the Bairu. By the use of such practices, with their surrounding magic and ceremony, the individual Mwiru might come to internalize the ideas about the correctness of his subordinate position held by the Bahima; to believe that his subordination was ordained by tradition and divine law; that he really was inferior, and that the Bahima were born to rule. He might pass on such notions to his children as they grew up. In such a way, the ideology of the dominant group might become widespread even among the dominated, a process which Marcuse tried to show was happening in the America of the 'fifties, and which we shall discuss further in Chapter 5 (Marcuse, 1964). Another source of potential conflict to the Bahima, a threat to their position derived from the external relations with other societies—was the *international structure*. If conquered, a Muhima, while retaining his privileges with regard to Bairu equivalents in surrounding societies, was nevertheless temporarily impoverished, and subject to arbitrary tribute by the conquerors. The threat of invasion was real enough to the Bairu, too, since if they were captured, they had their ears cut off and became slaves, the ultimate degradation. This tended to link them to the Bahima, who, because they were the only ones to possess weapons, were the only ones who could protect them from such a fate. In fact, the continual warfare can be seen to reduce the risk of internal conflict for all the societies in the area, as the threat of slavery for all in the position of a Mwiru led them to depend on those who could provide protection against this risk. Nevertheless, the succession ritual of Ankole becomes more intelligible if seen in terms of this second source of potential conflict. Although important concessions to favouritism are made in terms of the privileged position of the favourite son, it ensured that the Bahima would be led by a military leader who had proved his worth in battle, and his ability to marshal forces by obtaining the support of sufficient Bahima allies in the internal wars to achieve success. The new king had no rivals to challenge his position. The succession ritual as a whole can be understood as the attempt over the centuries of the Bahima to safeguard themselves against the external threat of invasion or raids, a threat deriving from the international organization of that area of Africa. The provision of great power to the king involves a further potential conflict; since the supplies required to maintain the king and his entourage were partly derived from the Bahima, they might need protection from that same power themselves. If a greater physical force were set above the king, the latter would be superfluous. The only way of attempting to control the controller was therefore in the realm of ideas. As in mediaeval Europe the king's power was not absolute but derived from God, so in Ankole the king's power was derived from the symbol of perfect kingship, the sacred drum, whose mystique, which all were aware of, involved the king in custom and ceremonial. The fact that the drum, insignia of kingship, was awarded by a powerful Muhima symbolized the derivation of the king's authority from this group, and the link between the religious symbol and the social basis of the society.

Problems of using the structural conflict approach in advanced societies

Ankole structure as described by Oberg was not too complex; its historical development, in as far as it could be ascertained, gave a clear guide to the structural relationships which enable us to understand the practices that had developed over the years in Ankole. Once again, we should emphasize that this method of analysis does not assume that Ankole practices were deliberately and consciously thought out by the Bahima in order to safeguard their position, although it is not impossible that some of the practices might have been. What are the problems of applying such a method of analysis to societies such as our own? The first of them is the complexity of modern literate societies, as compared to societies like the Ankole. It is not a question of having too little material—inadequate written records—but too much, containing so many diverse opinions. The task of singling out the key groups, and the basis, extent and development of dominance—that is, subordination relationships between them—is not an easy one. Where reality itself is really complex, the difficulty of the problem is often increased by the fact that some

63

sociologists seem to try to evade the necessity of studying the complexity of reality by developing complexity of terminology instead. Their language itself becomes convoluted and tangled, as if in an attempt to parallel the problems of the real world without ever meeting them:

> The conditions of manipulative complementarity and transactional co-operation illustrate an alternative to evoking or establishing consonance that is open for the goal originator. This alternative, of course, consists of wittingly or unwittingly 'paying off' others for becoming involved in the institutionalized pattern subserving the originating goal. For the others who become implicated in the interpersonal pattern under these conditions, the activity presents a round about route toward their own extraneous, presumably valent, specified and subjectively legitimate goals. But even assuming that these extraneous goals are unproblematic for the persons holding them, there must exist, (with certain exceptions) at least a minimal degree of consonance with respect to the originating goal, for them to become involved in the pattern directed toward it (Zollschan and Perucci, 1964).

In the last century, Engels once observed of the Hegelian school:

> It ... was limited to ... a compilation of words and turns of speech which had no other purpose than to be at hand at the right time where thought and positive knowledge were lacking. Thus ... these Hegelians understood nothing about anything, but could write about everything ... These gentlemen were, in spite of their sufficiency, so conscious of their weakness that they gave big problems the widest berth possible (Engels, 1958).

Many of the sociologists we are criticizing have hardly heard of Hegel, but otherwise the comment fits perfectly.

A second problem arises from the sociologist's membership of the society he is analysing. It is difficult for someone who is part of something to stand *apart* from it, and analyse it as a whole (Elias, 1956). All of us are bound up in the beliefs and ways of thinking we have absorbed since our childhood, and this pressures us towards looking at problems in certain ways, and tending to disregard others. It means that our personal relations, even our jobs, are involved in the kind of thinking we do—problems that were examined in the first chapter. It would be the greatest of mistakes, however, to believe that only one unified way of thinking prevails in our society, as it tends to in undeveloped societies such as the Arapesh. There are many traditions and sources to choose from, even if, among different groups at different times, some are more popular than others.

The third, and perhaps the major problem about the application of sociological analysis, that is, dynamic structural conflict analysis, to our societies, is that such analysis involves us in the great political and social issues of the day. It involves us in the attempt to analyse, as scientifically as we can, problems about which there may be systematic or non-systematic distortions in terms of available information; problems the investigation of which may be felt by some powerful groups to threaten their interests. It is not difficult for us to examine the situation in Ankole dispassionately, since we are not directly involved in that society, and its forms of organization are rapidly becoming a part of history. But imagine the effect of the publication of such an analysis in Ankole itself, in the local language, in the heyday of the social structure described. Doubtless, large sections of the Bahima would see the very publication of the analysis, the very asking of those questions, as a threat to their positions. Suppose the Bairu were to get hold of it—might the explicit recognition of their position of subordination in the society not encourage them to wish to change it? The publication of a structural analysis of Ankole society in such circumstances becomes a political act, one which might very well lead to the removal of the head of the author. There is no doubt also that, in analysing our own societies, there are social pressures to keep off the analysis of 'difficult' matter, to confine one's attention to subordinate problems—although our argument has been that a scientific analysis of subordinate problems in sociological terms depends on the use of the best available conception of the overall structure of the society—or to express oneself in terms so abstract that no specific existing society is examined at all.

It has been frequently argued that for some or all of these reasons, the structural conflict analysis is 'unscientific', and that concern should be directed to more easily manageable, small scale problems. We have tried to show on the other hand, that it is not only the best method of approaching sociological analysis, but the indispensable method.

In an historical structural analysis of our own societies, some facts emerge as crucial—for instance, the ownership and distribution of the wealth on which the society's existence is based. Such analyses would certainly be central to a sociological examination of our own society; but, for all the material there is, it has not been a central research focus for our sociologists (Miliband, 1969, Riddell, 1969). We are not trying to say that this kind of research alone, but this at least is necessary to the understanding of our society. It is not our job here to attempt to carry out a structural analysis of British or any other society—it would take a much larger volume—but to explain the necessity for, and some of the principles of such analyses, and indicate some of the reasons why they are not carried out as they should be. Perhaps one of the reasons for the appeal of functionalism and its derivatives becomes clearer. By

having an extra-historical, extra-social principle of analysis
—the maintenance of order—functionalists are enabled to
avoid the knotty problem of involvement, in the name of a
spurious objectivity.

4

Social change

The inadequacy of order and change as principles of analysis

If we reject some extra-social principle by which to explain social phenomena—for instance, the idea that there is some principle of order, by which all social events can be understood—we are forced instead to examine social groups in their positions in social structures. This examination involves considering the groups in interaction over time, so that all sociological analysis must be, to an extent, historical and dynamic. Of course, for reasons we have already outlined, in a sociology which is dominated by functionalist types of approach, we can expect many studies that ignore this dynamic element, and indeed we do find them. But they all in fact smuggle in assumptions about the past of the events they try to account for, and since these assumptions are not examined, all such studies are fundamentally unscientific, no matter what grand pretensions to rigorous methodology they may have.

A group of writers have been critical of functionalism and its variants because, they argue, it has ignored the obvious fact, obvious if one considers the societies of the world as a whole over the past two thousand years or so, that social change, both of the subordinate parts of social structures, and of the forms of whole social structures, has been continuous and universal. Perhaps the main advocate of this view has been a German sociologist, Ralf Dahrendorf, who sets out his criticisms in a most stimulating article, *Out of Utopia* (1964). These writers are quite correct as far as they go, but because they fail to challenge the logical fallacies of attributing some kind of supra-social motives to society, such as the maintenance of order, they tend to fall into the same fallacies in an opposite way, by asserting that there is some mysterious thing about society which makes it change all the time, unless something stops it. So Dahrendorf says:

> A Galilean change of thought is required which makes us realize that all units of social organization are continuously changing, unless some force intervenes to arrest this change.

As you can see, this assertion is as baseless as its opposite, but it has led many writers to suggest that there is a choice in sociology, one which depends to a considerable extent on the temperament of the student—if you are an easy-going sort of chap, you will probably like an approach based on order, while dynamic, bustling fellows are going to prefer change. Cohen, a British writer, prefers order for four completely spurious and unexamined reasons (Cohen, 1968, p. 18, paragraph 1—try to see why they are spurious); Chinoy considers a little of both to be necessary (Chinoy, 1967, Ch. 5, 'Modes of Sociological Analysis' —a chapter full of all the mistakes we have been describing with regard to the use of the word society); while Inkeles, recognizing that different approaches alter the results, nevertheless refuses to evaluate them (Inkeles, 1964, Ch. 4, p. 34-39).

The whole point is that any statement about order or

change in a society depends on an analysis of the interactions of groups in the social structure of that society.
In other words, a structural-historical analysis will enable
us to explain both order and its absence and change and its
absence. There are many examples of research which came
to grief because of false ideas as to how to set about the
task, and a lack of structural historical approach. In one
famous case, Elton Mayo and his researchers, working on
the Hawthorne studies in an American factory, heard in
twenty-thousand interviews in which numerous grievances
were expressed, no criticism of the management of the
firm, yet the research ended in an atmosphere of bitterness
as many workers at the plant were declared redundant
(Horowitz, 1963, Blumberg, 1968, ch. 2, 3). In a more
recent case, a team of British sociologists who ought to
have known better, spent a great deal of time and effort
concocting theories as to why the workers at the Vauxhall
car factory were so orderly, barely a month after the
publication of which the plant was subject to some of the
most violent strikes of recent times in the British motor
industry (Blackburn, 1967, p. 48-50). American sociologists
have been rightly criticized for failing to predict or understand the so-called 'race-riots' (socio-economic uprisings?)
in the Black ghettoes of American cities, (Baran and
Sweezy, 1968, Ch. 9, Silberman, 1964) while endless
volumes written to explain the stability of 'advanced',
'democratic' societies have been deflated by the events in
France in May, 1968 (c.f., Mandel, 1968). Endless studies
in so-called political sociology are devoted to trying to
show that we can learn significant things about politics in
a society on the basis of the expressed preferences of voters
on day X of month Y of year Z (c.f. Samuel, 1960). Incidentally, in the first Russian revolution of 1905, Leon
Trotsky, its main leader, saw the circulation of his newspaper rise from 500 to 300,000 in a month (Trotsky, 1960,
p. 177). In 1917, when the previously banned Pravda, Bol-

shevik newspaper, reappeared, its second issue sold 100,000 copies (Carr, 1966, p. 84). A sociology which enables us to explain and predict such changes is a science of society; much of what passes for sociology is pseudo-science, in spite of its pretensions, because its basic approach is fallacious.

It follows that sociologists do not need just to pay a little more attention to change, or even a lot more, nor do they need to make change, as opposed to order, their basis of analysis. Rather they need to make groups of people in interaction over time in social structures their basis of analysis. Unfortunately, many of the ideas that are common in much British and American sociology derive from static types of analysis, and are therefore themselves inadequate (as are many of the current methods—for instance, opinion and attitude sampling by means of sample surveys may seem rigorous in its design, but, since it is essentially an a-historical method, it has very limited application in scientific sociology [Cicourel, 1964]). This is one of the reasons why we have suggested that a lot of sociological analysis parallels the complexity of social reality by the complexity of its language, rather than explaining it. If we are concerned with the interrelations over time of groups of people in social structures, then we are trying to understand *processes from interactions in structures*. This is a dialectical analysis; our argument is that by a theory of the structured dialectics of social situations, based on historical investigation, we shall best be able to explain such processes and predict how they will develop. The necessity to analyse social phenomena in this way makes it considerably more difficult to use exact mathematical techniques in large areas of sociology, but the use of such techniques is often spurious anyway, the scientific form being substituted for the scientific reality. This is not to attack the use of mathematics in sociology—but to argue that the problem and appropriate method must determine what mathematical techniques can be used—not the other way round.

The title of this chapter is social change; so far, we have criticized the incorrect approaches which have led, in much sociology, to underemphasis of explanation of social change. We have argued that it is a mistake to separate change and order in such a way that one can choose to base sociological explanation on either the former or the latter. It is equally mistaken to select sometimes one type of explanation, sometimes another type, depending on whether the immediate concern is to understand why something persists or why it does not. Our argument is that a sociological perspective based on historical structural analysis is necessary so that we can explain persistence *and* change *and* the relations between them. This approach must be dynamic, not static. Further, just as we argued previously that the behaviour of individuals or groups can only be understood within the context of social structures, so, when studying social changes, the explanation of small scale changes in a society cannot be divorced from their relationship to the total organization of the society, in its historical development.

We also want to argue that the kinds of interactions which provide the major basis for the sociological explanation of structural change in societies are those in which different groups, in different positions in the structure, come into conflict. To use jargon, conflict, realized or potential, is integral to the dialectics of social change, although it is not their only basis. Let us imagine a highly simplified society, in which there are two major groups, x and y.

In social structure A, x and y are not in a conflict relationship. What sources of change are there?

1. By pressure from representatives of an outside society. (This source of change—or external pressure to resist

internal change—is absolutely crucial in the approach to the sub-discipline of sociology which goes by the name of the sociology of development.)

2. By necessity as a result of natural events which cannot be controlled by the groups.
3. By mutual agreement of the groups. (This does not mean that the resulting change will benefit both groups equally—one group might misjudge the implications of a change, and lose out to the other group as a result.)

Let us now suppose that a structural change has occurred as a result of either 1, 2, or 3, which puts group x in a superior structural position as defined by some objectively verifiable criterion to group y. We now have social structure B.

In social structure B, x and y are in a potential conflict relationship as a result of x's structural superiority. What sources of social change are there? 1, 2, 3 still exist, but there are two new ones:

4. The use by group x of its superior structural position to impose change on group y (this might be by coercion or persuasion as we shall discuss in the next chapter).
5. The reaction by group y to its inferior position in relation to group x.

Since an examination of most of the world's societies shows that they approximate more to social structure type B than to type A (though their structures are usually much more complex than in this simple example), and since changes 1, 2, 3 more often than not lead away from type A structures towards type B structures, we are therefore justified in concluding that conflict, which is implied by 4 and 5, and usually by 1 as well, is integral to social change, as we asserted above. Notice that the way that the model is laid out seems to suggest conscious decisions by the members of the groups involved. If we examine societies historically, however, this is not by any means always the case. As has been pointed out earlier, some decisions are taken consciously; some seem to the participants to 'happen', since they derive from structural pressures which the participants themselves don't understand, or are mystified about; some are a mixture of both; other decisions may have consequences different from those intended. Writers who argue that type 4 sources of change are conscious decisions have been scathingly labelled 'conspiracy theorists' by some sociologists. Whether a change from source 4 is wholly or partly due to a conspiracy among members of group x can only be determined by the actual study of the circumstances involved, which is often very difficult, since groups who do not wish it to be known what they are deciding are hardly likely to be frank with sociologists or to leave easily available records (Mills, 1959b, part 1).

Let us now take an actual example of a study of social change, as a basis for further discussion. Again, we are using an example from social anthropology, for the same reasons as before, namely, that it is less complex in some ways than the study of our own society, and also because we are less involved in it. Kathleen Gough studied changes in family relationships among the Nayars of the Malabar coast of India (Gough, 1952). The basis of her study is not merely interviews with villagers from the area, but a careful examination of written records about this society, dating as far back as the sixteenth century.

The Nayars live on the south-west Indian coast, part of the population of the area known as the Malabar coast. They were a caste grouping in the kingdoms of Calicut and Cochin, that is, a group of the population recruited by birth, whose distinctiveness was based on the general type of occupations they held, and sanctioned by religious beliefs and practices which had grown up over a long period. (For additional discussion of caste, see Cox, 1959, part 1.) The organization of the Nayar family was based on a family group, centred round the mother; that is, property and inheritance came through the mother and not through the father, whose property, etc., went to his sister's children. This kind of family system anthropologists call a matrilineal kinship system, and it has the effect of weakening relationships between the family created by marriage, and strengthening those on the mother's side of the family a person is born into. Also, the Nayars were both polyandrous and polygynous. That is, a woman normally had several husbands, and a man several wives. If a man were staying with one of his wives for the night, he would leave his weapons outside her door, to indicate to her other husbands, of whom there might be seven or eight, that he was within. Husbands had very few obligations to their wives, who were supported by their maternal family group. The paternity of children was usually uncertain, and divorce was a mere formality. In addition to these tenuous husbands, a woman was ritually married to one of an appropriate group of Nayar men when she was very young, although this ritual marriage gave the husband neither obligations to her, nor rights over her. It simply established a woman's eligibility for other husbands. The problem for sociologists is to explain the reasons for this interesting family system, and for its subsequent changes. Gough searches for explanation in the development of the structural organization of the Kingdoms where the Nayars lived, and their relations with surrounding societies. Over a period of time, as a caste system of society develops, a group of the population becomes specialized in a type of occupation which becomes hereditary, so that a person cannot marry someone from another caste—a fisherman could marry a fisherman's daughter, for example, but never a pot maker's daughter. The system is also heirarchical, so that some jobs are, in belief and religion, better than others, and worthy of more social reward. The dangers of protest and revolt by those who suffer under this system at the expense of those at the top are minimized by the theology, which teaches that a good, obedient member of a low caste may be reborn into a higher caste, but that someone who protests may find himself reborn as an animal or insect. Since people in all castes were taught to believe this implicitly from childhood, it provided a very effective means of resisting change, especially since the caste trained in the use of weapons was near the top of the hierarchy. The Nayars were such a military group. But in a caste system, to have a hereditarily based military group creates certain problems, for, if warriors become too attached to their wives and children, they may not be so keen to fight—on the other hand, they are the only source of new warriors, since no woman from the military caste may have intercourse with someone from outside the caste. It is very likely indeed that the Nayar family system developed as a solution to this problem. Through the maternal family group, mothers could be provided for and children brought up, while older men and women, as well as tenant serfs, could cultivate lands collectively belonging to the group. The multiple husband-wife marriage system meant that a man could create children, satisfy sexual desires, without having any strong obligations either to his wife or to his children which might have made him reluctant to fight. This view is strengthened by the fact that in adjacent northern kingdoms where Nayars fought only intermittently for different chiefs and owned their land, polyandry was unknown.

At the end of the eighteenth century, British controlled forces with superior organization and weaponry conquered the Rajah's armies, and imposed British rule over the area. Thus, in terms of our previous model, a source one change took place. The Rajah's armies were disbanded, the Nayar soldiers returned to their family groups, and almost immediately the polyandrous system of Nayar marriages died out, indicating its close link with the Nayars' structural position. It would be a mistake to explain this change in purely military terms, however. The British acted neither from a desire to show their military might, nor from a wish to 'civilize the natives', but because political control made the export of India's wealth to Britain easier. In the fifty years between 1750 and 1800, between £100 and £150 million of India's wealth at least was transferred to Britain, wealth which was an important help in providing the capital necessary for Britain's industrial revolution in the nineteenth century (Mandel, 1968a, p. 443).

As the young Nayar men returned home and began to cultivate their fields themselves, to pay more attention to wives and children, they were subjected to conflicting loyalties to their own children and to their sisters'; to their own wives, and to the demands of their maternal relatives. Since the matrilineal system was now no longer related to the Nayars' position in the social structure, the conflict was between the new position of the Nayar males, and old traditions and customs, which slowly began to decline. As the century went on, the British introduced roads and railways, so that British goods, now being produced in huge quantities in the North of England could be easily sold, incidentally destroying the local handicraft production of India, and thus determining India's development into a backward country (Barratt-Brown, 1963, p. 41f., 174f.). At the same time, plantations for tea, coffee, and rubber were opened up by Europeans so that the natural wealth of the land might also be exported. Labour for these jobs was not recruited on a closed caste basis, and cash wages, small as they were, meant that a money economy increased in importance. Since the Nayars' matrilineal family system was linked to the caste system, as the latter was eroded, so the decay of the former was speeded up, and through the nineteenth and early twentieth centuries, the nuclear family (father, mother, children) was developing at the expense of the matrilineal family group.

This example illustrates several important points. First of all, the key to understanding the changes that took place within the Nayar family lies in the effects on the local social structure of a source one change, the British intervention. Secondly, the changes in the Nayar family system were not intended or planned by the British—they were an indirect result of the British satisfying their economic interests at India's expense (although not all Indians suffered equally—as is often, indeed usually the case, those in subordinate positions in the social stucture suffered most). Thirdly, the major explanation of the changes cannot be found in the influence of European ideas—about monogamy, or the inheritance of property from father to son, for example; as Gough is careful to point out, other European ideas, Christianity, for example, had almost no impact on the Nayars. Thus, in this case, an *idealist* explanation of the changes is not upheld (in sociology, idealism is used to mean a theory which explains things as being caused by ideas).

Approaches to the study of social change

We are now perhaps in a better position to examine some of the approaches to the explanation of social change which are current in sociology, using, where appropriate, examples and models we have already introduced into the text (Gerth & Mills, 1954, Ch. 13 is useful for reference here). As we pointed out right at the beginning of the book, the extent to which this subject is studied at all, especially at introductory level, varies from country to country and school to school of sociology, but since it is our contention that there is no separate study of social change, no separate subject at all, the discussion ought to be part of basic sociology. If you agree, but it isn't on your course, find the reason why.

In explaining the reasons for the disappearance of polyandrous marriage among the Nayars, Gough gives weight to one factor—the disbanding of the Rajah's armies by the imposition of British control. Explanations of social change which stress one factor are often called *monistic*, while theories of social change which say that all social change is due to one factor are called monistic theories. Suppose Gough had tried to list every possible factor in accounting for the disappearance of polyandry. Probably the list would have been very long. An attempt to explain social change in terms of all the possible factors is called *pluralistic*, and theories of social change which stress large numbers of factors are called pluralistic. This distinction is worth examining in more detail, because there have been a lot of arguments about whether explanations in terms of one factor are of any value. As is often the case, the easiest way to sort out the problem is to take a hypothetical example.

We are trying to explain social change X. Let us suppose that 100 represents a perfect explanation, and that a perfect explanation involves five factors, *a, b, c, d, e.* Out of the 100 making a perfect explanation, *a* accounts for 80, *b, c, d, e*, for five each. In a perfect explanation of social change Y, on the other hand, *a* accounts for 50, *b* for 30, *c* and *d* for 8 each, and *e* for only 4. In a perfect explanation of social change Z, each of the five factors, *a, b, c, d, e* accounts for 20.

For social change X, if we were to ignore factors *b, c, d, e*, we should still have a good explanation, though not a perfect one. For social change Y, if we were to ignore *b, c, d, e*, we should have a reasonable explanation, and have picked out the most important factor, *a*. If we single out *a* and *b*, we shall have a good explanation, and the two main factors. For social change Z, we should have to have at least *a, b, c*, to get a reasonable explanation, and even if we had *a, b, c, d*, we should be ignoring one main factor, *e*.

Obviously, considering the difficulties of sociological research, for social change X, a monistic explanation would
be very satisfactory for most purposes. For Y, it would be
satisfactory, and a two factor explanation very satisfactory. For Z, only a pluralistic explanation would do. It is
therefore nonsense for sociologists to assert that only pluralistic explanations of social change will do, unless most
social changes in the real world are similar to type Z; in
fact it is much more correct in terms of all the research
that has been done, to say that most explanations of social
change resemble those of X and Y. It is therefore wrong
to assert that pluralism is necessary for reasonable
explanation of prediction of most social changes.

So far, our hypothetical example has been presented in
statistical terms, that is, statically, and as if all the explaining factors were separate. It is more difficult, but a better
approximation to reality, to present the example *dialectically*, that is, with the factors in interaction over time. Let
us take social change Y. In the previous example, factor a
was 50, b—30, c and d—8, and e—4, in terms of their
contribution to the total explanation of the change. But
now a must be expressed as the composite factor a, the
total of (a influenced by b, a by c, a by d, a by e), composite factor b, the total of (b influenced by a, b by c, b by d,
b by e), and so on. A similar pattern will apply for social
change Z. In other words, the 'true' isolated factors disap-
pear, and what we have are factors 'contaminated' by other
factors. In reality, the 'true' factors never occur, and so all
factors are really 'contaminated' ones. But there is still
an important difference between social changes Y and Z.
For, in the case of Z, all the interactions will be of equal
explanatory importance, while in the case of Y, the influence of factor a on factor c will be greater than that of c
on a, and so on. In the latter case, we have a hierarchy of
interactions. We can therefore say that, if the process of
interactions leading to Z is a *dialectic*, the process of inter-

actions leading to Y is a *structured dialectic*, and we can substitute these terms for pluralism and monism respectively, in the static model.

We argued that there was no separate theory for social change and for social order. If, instead of our factors a, b, c, d, e, being considered as positive reasons for change, we consider some of them as reasons for lack of it, then the result of the interactions will tell us whether X Y or Z is a structural change or not. For instance, if we combine the examples and consider X as the disappearance of polyandry among the Nayars, then factor a becomes the British control of the society in dominance over factor b, the Rajah's control. But, if factor b had been stronger than factor a, i.e., if the Rajah had defeated the British, polyandry would probably have continued to exist. The dialectical approach can therefore be seen to be not merely appropriate for the explanation of social change, but the method for all structural sociological explanation.

It is now possible to continue our examination of approaches to social change. We will take a hypothetical example, relating it to reality. Suppose we had 100 cases of type X or Y social changes. If in all of them, or a large proportion of them, the main factor was similar, we should begin to think that we had discovered a very important aid to our studies, for, in spite of the differences between the problems, we should have a line of approach that would be very helpful. Many social theorists have argued that no such aid exists, that every case has to be studied entirely afresh, that there are no 'laws of history' (Popper, 1957). Of course, if we say that a 'law' means that something must always invariably happen, this is probably true, but if we talk rather of trends, of guides to approach, it is much less plausible to deny them (Bottomore, 1963, Ch. 2, Taylor, 1958, Novack, 1968). In fact, many sociologists have posited such aids, and their propositions fall into three great categories.

81

Into the category of *idealism* fall those theories which put forward the view that the source of social changes lies most importantly in men's minds, in the sorts of ideas that they have. Auguste Comte took this view, as does David McClelland today (Mill, 1866, McClelland, 1961). It is not plausible, for if it were true, ideas would occur at random, independent of place and circumstance, and social change follow from them. As we shall see in the next chapter, and have already discussed to some extent in Chapter 2, human beings are dependent on social training for the very language they use, so the absolute independence of ideas is not upheld (MacIntyre, 1966, Ch. 1, Gerth & Mills, 1954, Ch. 10, Frank, 1967b).

Those theories which attribute the major source of change to material changes, usually of technology, we can call *mechanical materialist*. Ludwig Feuerbach took this view, and Hart and Leslie Whyte are modern representatives (Engels, 1958, Whyte, 1949, Hart, 1959). It is true that the material world existed before man came on the scene, but once he is there, the decision to introduce any technology is a human one, though it may have unforseen consequences. The technology *alone* cannot be considered the key explanatory factor (c.f., Gerth & Mills, 1954, Ch. 13).

Theories of *dialectical materialism* argue that it is in the relations that men enter into in order to produce and appropriate the wealth of a society that the major key to the explanation of structural social change may be found. Marx developed this kind of approach. Some modern exponents are Baran and Sweezy (1968), Frank (1967a), and Mandel (1968a). This kind of theory is structural and sociological, but, if misapplied can end up as a sort of dogmatics, providing a mechanical formula by which every social change is explained, without the need to study at all. This kind of distortion has often been called economic determinism, or 'vulgar marxism', and has been practised on a large scale by so-called Marxists, most notably those connected with the bureaucratically based elites of the Soviet Union (Marcuse, 1968b). In the context of the cold war, and with the implications which Marx's theories predict for the destinies of those groups now controlling our societies, the view that dialectical materialism means simple economic determinism has been widely propagated and believed. It is not correct. The reader is invited to read two articles by Marx, *The Civil War in France*, and *The Eighteenth Brumaire of Louis Napoleon*, to see how he applied dialectical materialism (Marx, 1958). Engels, Marx's close collaborator, wrote :

> The economic situation is the basis, but the various elements of the superstructure—the political forms of the class struggle and its results: to wit constitutions established by the victorious classes after a successful battle, etc., juridical forms, and then even the reflexes of all these actual struggles in the brains of the participants, political, juristic, philosophical theories, religious views, and their further development into systems of dogmas—also exercise their influence upon the course of the historical struggles, and in many cases predonderate in determining their form (Engels, Letter to Bloch in Marx-Engels, 1958).

A very important and careful formulation of dialectical materialism has been made by Althusser (1967). Although his language is difficult, in our view it repays study because, instead of just paralleling the complexity of the real world, it does help us to understand it. To emphasize that dialectical materialism is not simple economic determinism, Althusser introduces the idea of *overdetermination*. This combines two propositions : that no factors of explanation can be isolated from their social structural context; and that, although the examination of relationships of production and appropriation of wealth is crucial, it is unlikely by itself to be adequate to a proper explanation of social change. He considers how such factors both determine and are determined, 'in one and the same movement by the various levels and instances of the social formation'; 'The economy is determinant (of social change) but only in the last instance'; however, 'The lonely hour of the "last instance" never comes.'

His argument—for detailed study of the whole situation in historical perspective in order to determine the major factors in their interrelation—means, in the terms we have used above, that most social changes are of type Y, rather than of type X or Z. Althusser illustrates his approach by a brief but masterly analysis of the Russian revolution, indicating the overdetermining factors on which it depended.

These three approaches are, in our view, the most significant attempts to provide a way in to the study of social change, by singling out a crucial key factor of the most general kind. It is clear from the text that we think such an attempt is valuable, and which approach we favour. But it is very important to understand that the merits of such approaches cannot be decided *a priori*; they derive from, and must be judged by the examination of social reality. Since these approaches are expressed in such broad terms, they cannot be refuted in any simple way, and, because of the complexity of most social phenomena, it is often possible for an investigator to single out those factors which seem to lend weight to the approach which he consciously, or subconsciously holds. As the political implications of different approaches are intertwined with all this, it becomes easy to understand why there is disagreement among sociologists. In the end, every student has to make judgments for himself. In our view, the best way of reaching such judgments is by comparison of studies of the same social problem by the different approaches, examining their logical construction, and their use of data.

Among other methods of trying to study social change,

two should be mentioned in this cursory examination, since in various forms they have considerable influence. Theories which maintain that the basis for sociological analysis is the maintenance of order are logically debarred from explaining social change (Rex, 1963). In trying to square this particular circle, functionalists have come up with the concept of 'structural differentiation', of which Neil Smelser is the main proponent (Smelser, 1960). This shows that the functions which one institution performs come, over time, to be spread among other institutions, differentiated. Thus, one form of social equilibrium is replaced by another, more complex one, with possibly a period of tension, disturbance in between. This approach is a prime example of a fault commonly found in studies of social change—it does not really explain what is happening, but merely describes it in a different way, so that a sleight of hand is involved. The method is also static, moving from one 'equilibrium' to another. When one asks for the reasons for the initial situation, and the reasons for the changes—why? questions—the whole façade collapses. Smelser's main example is change in the cotton industry in the British industrial revolution. The reader is invited to compare it with a dialectical materialist interpretation by E. P. Thompson, remembering that the latter writer is an historian, not a sociologist, and thus tends not to lay out clearly his principles of analysis, which remain implicit (Thompson, 1963).

There is a vast amount of literature on the sociology of 'development'—the study of underdevelopment, which contains a large amount of the poorest writing in sociology, and a little of the best. A common theme in this, in one form or another, is that of 'modernization' in which a writer from an 'advanced' society, usually American, tries to explain why an underdeveloped society is not like his own, or how it might become more like his own (e.g., Lerner, 1964). Such approaches involve a basic sociological fault called *ethnocentrism*, that is, they judge another society or group by standards and practices current in their own. That the underdeveloped society has a historically dynamic structure of its own, and that this structure has been affected, often for centuries, by interactions of an international nature, is thus ignored. In no area of sociology is ideological commitment so powerful a determinant of scholarship as this, and Frank has examined the field in a brilliant and devastating article, *The Sociology of Development and the Underdevelopment of Sociology*, unfortunately printed in a rather obscure journal (Frank, 1967b, see also Rhodes, 1968).

In this chapter, we have put forward the view that the study of social change is not an appendage, tagged on to the 'main study', nor yet that it is *the* principle by which societies should be examined, but rather that, since historical structural analysis provides the sociological approach which explains change and order, our material develops logically out of the previous chapter. We argued for the necessity of a dynamic, rather than a static approach, and an appropriate language. We tried to show the close relationship of structural conflict to structural social change, attacked pluralism as a principle, while defending a structured dialectic approach, and in terms of the discussion of key factors, supported dialectical materialism. The key area remaining is the relationship between structure and human action, and it is under the heading of 'social consciousness' that we propose to examine this.

5

Social consciousness

Social consciousness and social structure

The following incident is recounted in Tom Johnston's wonderful *History of the Working Classes in Scotland*:

> At Ballindalloch, on the Spey, a poor man had been sentenced to death, and the gallows not being ready he was put in the baron's pit while the scaffold was being erected. At length everything was in order, and the baron's men called upon the prisoner to come up; but instead of coming up the doomed man drew a sword and threatened to slay the first individual who came down for him. Persuasion and threat were equally unavailing, until at last, the victim's wife appeared and cried: 'Come up quietly and be hangit, Donal', and dinna anger the laird' (Johnston, 1929, p. 47).

For Donal's wife, clearly the peace of mind of the laird meant more than her relationship to Donal'. At the opposite pole, the fighters of the National Liberation Front of the southern part of the poor peasant country of Vietnam have for several years kept at bay, and are coming close to defeating, the forces of the world's most powerful nation, the United States, forces comprising 42 per cent of its entire land forces, 58 per cent of its marines, 32 per cent of all its fighter planes, 60 per cent of its aircraft carriers, dropping 64,000 tons of bombs a month, involving an expenditure of some 97,000 million dollars in the last four years. Although some have argued that these successes are due to terrorism, it is our considered opinion that, in fact, they are the result of a degree of determination and conviction which can rarely have been matched in world history; this struggle has had considerable repercussions in the West (Therborn, 1968). In either example, the way in which structural conflicts are worked out is heavily dependent on the *consciousness* of the participants, and we may assume that this is generally the case.

Many structuralist sociologists, particularly of the functional type, have tended to under emphasize or even ignore the importance of the social consciousness of the participants in determining actual courses of events. Even Marx himself never gave sufficient attention to the problem, although he always made clear in his approach that the consciousness of the members of a social class of belonging to that class was a prerequisite for joint action by the class to change a social structure, and scattered ideas in his writings provide the basis from which a structuralist theory of social consciousness might be constructed (Ossowski, 1963).

At the time of writing, there is a reaction among some sociologists against the neglect of social consciousness in much functionalist theory, and its under emphasis in much Marxist-oriented theory, a reaction which has led to a new interest in the work of such social psychologists as G. H. Mead and Irving Goffman, who emphasize the importance of interactions of people in small groups in developing their images of themselves, others and society generally (Mead, G., 1934, Goffman, 1959). In studies in the peculiarly named sub-field called the sociology of deviancy, there have been interesting investigations not into the social background of the deviants, but into the ways in which interactions with people in other social positions create and reinforce the definition of a person as a 'deviant', even to himself (e.g., MacIntosh, 1968, Becker, 1964).

The dangers of this approach, valuable though it is, are in the fallacy known as *reductionism*, and are expressed in the popular phrase, 'it's all in the mind', i.e., that the examination of all social phenomena can be reduced to the examination of the views of the situation held by the individual participants. In the same way that we tried to establish earlier that a social structure is more than the sum of its parts, so we must establish that a social structure is more than the sum of the individual consciousnesses of its participants—but that it is *not* a sort of collective consciousness. If we know that, say three quarters of the people in a society hold a certain view at a particular time, this does not necessarily tell us what the social structure is. Thus we are arguing against the views:

1. that social structure totally determines social consciousness, and
2. that social consciousness totally determines social structure, and
3. that social structure and social consciousness are unrelated, independent.

The best way to describe the relationship between the two is of the form we described in the last chapter as a structured dialectic, i.e., their relationship is a process of interactions, of which the structural component is of greater weight. In the last chapter we used a hypothetical example to indicate the relations between factors in explaining a social phenomenon; we found that a static model was inadequate—that we had to have a dynamic, or dialectical model. The introduction of the idea of social consciousness brings a further complication. Social consciousness is, in one sense, just one of the factors to be considered in explanation; but it is also more than this, for all social phenomena involve the behaviour and interaction of people; thus social consciousness is an intervening variable in *every* social situation. While other factors may or may not be present in an explanation, social consciousness always is. This chapter attempts to explore some of the implications of this particular dialectical relationship.

It is fairly easy to give examples to refute the proposition made by one leading British social theorist recently that social structure exists only 'in the head of the participants' (McIntyre, 1969). King Canute showed his sycophantic courtiers that all his power and determination could not keep back the waves; in a social structure in which the organization of an adequate technology has not been developed, all men's efforts, say, to fly are doomed to failure; we previously gave an example of the difference between the demand for printing apprenticeships and the actual number, which is determined by factors outside the demand to a large extent—thus, however much the applicants desire to become printing apprentices, believe they can become printing apprentices, some of them will be disappointed; however much an American believes that he has a chance of becoming President, it is clearly impossible for every American to become President; even if the aspirant is a white millionaire with a business background and a high position in a political party machine, his chances are very low indeed, while if his skin happens to be black in colour, they are rather less than those of King Canute in keeping back the tide! However much a man believes a social structure to be unjust, or that an usurping social group should and can be overthrown, it is very unlikely that he on his own can achieve this end—unless social conditions are such that his views come to seem reasonable to a sufficient number of other people. Thus the idea that social structure is independent of, or totally determined by social consciousness is clearly shown to be implausible. But, to continue with our last example, whatever the contradictions inherent in a social structure, there is no law that it will automatically be transformed without the conscious intervention of organized groups of the population, as some vulgar Marxists have inferred, or indeed that the social consciousness of underprivileged groups will come to express automatically and coherently their position in the social structure, an even more common fallacy. Nevertheless, the structural influences on position are powerful. To revert to the example of collective consciousness among working class people mentioned in another connection in chapter two, structurally, any individual worker is in a very poor position to advance his interests on his own. He is much less powerful than the individual employer. Only if he acts collectively in solidarity with his fellows is he likely to make gains. Hence the fear of early employers to accept the organization of workers into trade unions, a fear still shared by many employers today, and the pressures on trade union leaders from employers and state not to act in solidarity with their members, but as mediators between workers and employers (Allen, 1966, ch. 1). The worker's structural position constantly reinforces this collectivist consciousness, at least in some aspects, but many other influences, notably those of the employer controlled mass media he uses, are much more individualistic in orientation, so that each generation of workers has, to some extent, to re-learn the experience of former ones, and the degree to which collective consciousness exists varies markedly from worker to worker and from factory to factory. Studies of workers in middle class occupations indicate that, whereas their structural position used to be such that their individual interests appeared to be best served by cultivating individually good relations with superiors, leading away from trade unionism, and to an extreme individualism in orientation to life, for some groups, especially in large institutions and mechanized offices, collectivism has come to seem more realistic, with the resulting growth of middle class trade unionism (Lockwood, 1958). Here, in order to make clearer what we are arguing, all these examples are presented as if they can be explained by a single factor. In reality, the explanations have the sort of complexity we described in the last chapter.

In an example also mentioned earlier, Bettleheim described the behaviour and attitudes of guards and inmates of a Nazi concentration camp. He found that not only did the guards come to regard the prisoners as sub-human vermin, to whom the most brutal behaviour was justified, but a proportion of prisoners came to accept, under the pressure, that they really were what the guards thought them to be, and behaved to each other as such. Bettleheim found that the prisoners who succumbed first and most readily to the guards' definition of them were those who held neither a deeply felt religious ideology, nor had a clearly worked out philosophy of man in society; evangelical christians and communists resisted more strongly than people whose religion was nominal or whose political affiliation nondescript. The interactions between prisoners and guards resulted in the adoption by one group of a self-image proposed by another; to understand why, however, we must know about the social structure of the camp, and about the historical development of the wider social structure, in two respects— firstly, what in the wider social structure was responsible for the narrower social structure of the camp, and secondly, what features of the wider social structure, via the socialization process, provided the basis for the different types of attitudes between the prisoners themselves (c.f., Goffman, 1968).

These examples have been used to indicate in different ways the structured dialectic of social structure and social consciousness. We can now go on to consider other aspects of this difficult but basic relationship.

Socialization

Social consciousness depends on learning, and the term we introduced earlier with regard to this was socialization. Many sociologists, especially those who tend in one way or another to fall into the fallacy of reification, agelicism, lay great stress on a crude 'one way' conception of socialization, in which an individual learns to do 'as society tells him'. In this conception, aspects of which have already been criticized, roles, provided by society, are learnt by an individual through the medium of his family, friends, etc., enabling him to become an adjusted, i.e., role-playing, member of society. One school of sociologists, commonly known as the culture-personality school, heavily influenced by psychoanalytic theories, regard early childhood experiences as the paramount influence, so that, lacking any conception of social structure, they claim to be able to identify characteristics of a 'national character', which they relate to early socialization procedures of young children. Thus, in one study, the 'Great Russian character' is claimed to be a mixture of repression and violent outbursts of aggression, deriving from the fact that Russian children are often swaddled when young (repression=being swaddled; violent outbursts=times when swaddling material is changed!). Studies in similar vein have been made of quite a number of societies, and readers who have followed our arguments so far will understand why we consider them to be thoroughly misconceived (Gorer and Richman, 1949, Kardiner, 1945). Useful critiques have been made by Orlansky (1949) and Lindesmith and Strauss (1950).

93

On the one-way conception of socialization a whole jargon can be built up, so that 'anticipatory' socialization occurs when a child in play 'rehearses' his adult roles, and socialization can be typed, according to the generality of the roles learned (e.g., British subject, worker, steel worker, furnaceman. C.f., Musgrave, 1967, Coulson, et. al., 1967). A deviant can then be defined as being for some reason inadequately socialized, and such individuals may give a means, otherwise denied to this kind of sociologist, of explaining social change. In exasperation at the mechanistic conception of man that this approach leads to, Wrong wrote an article entitled, *The Oversocialized Conception of Man in Modern Sociology*, in which he shows that the formulation of the society—individual relation as a one-way adaptation depends on the consensus view of society: 'The oversocialized view of man is a counterpart of the over-integrated view of society.' (Wrong, 1964.) These two basic mistakes—and it is important to recognize that they depend upon one another—make much of the subordinate theorizing of little value.

What we should be examining in a discussion of the development of social consciousness, socialization, is not a one-way relationship between society and individual, but a structured dialectic of pressures deriving from structural situations interacting with the existing consciousness of an individual. While, once again, the language of interaction and process is not translatable into statistical terms in the same way as the language of a static one-way model, it represents reality, and is not a gross distortion of it. The way such relationships can be conceptualized and studied has been shown in a lifetime series of researches about child development by Jean Piaget, on the boundaries of psychology and sociology, in which the development of some of the most basic components of consciousness is examined. Any new experience, *a*, he argues, will be *assimilated* to the existing consciousness, X, of the individual; it will be accounted for within that consciousness—in terms of an outside criterion, will be distorted by it to become a^1. But the existing consciousness will also *accommodate* itself to the experience, be affected by it to become X^1. Another experience, b, will, by the interaction of b and X^1, be interpreted as b^1, while X^1 becomes X^2, and so on. When we realize that experiences can be of different importance, so that modification X^2 might be bigger than X^1, for instance, we can imagine how complex this process of interaction can become (Piaget, 1953).

Only with this kind of approach can sociology do justice to the complexity, apparent contradictoriness, and individuality that human beings display. It is not just that sociologists have tried to explain too much by the concept of socialization; their principle of explanation has been inadequate. This has led to a general underestimation of the potentiality of human individuals for change in appropriate structural conditions, and provides a general ideological background for elitist, manipulative and conservative political views. This restrictive conception of human potentiality is not confined to sociology. Leading elites tend to justify their positions by regarding the 'mass' as dull-witted and incapable of initiative, so that when people do act in resistance to various injustices, e.g. workers striking, this is interpreted as being 'engineered' by 'agitators', 'professional revolutionaries', etc. As we write, the *Times* has declared that there are special organizers working among Catholics and Protestants in the fighting in the northern part of Ireland, and that the Derry citizens' street-fighting techniques have been learned from groups of student revolutionaries who have come over from France to teach them (*Times*, 13/8/69).

The process of socialization in any complex social structure is such that potentialities for action and development in many directions are available to individuals, once appropriate structural opportunities are also made available. An example from a study in Poland may illustrate this (Pomianowsky, 1959). It has been observed from many countries that the attendance of working class people at theatres is very low, of the order of 3 per cent of the group. The more 'difficult' a play is, the less the interest. In a new steel making town, Nowa Huta, a theatre was built. The new company made no concessions to the new audience, putting on some of the world's avant-garde plays in the most avant-garde presentation. In a short time, a survey revealed 36 per cent of the population of the town as regular theatregoers; a parallel investigation in the old city of Cracow, with seven theatres and a great cultural tradition, revealed a figure of between 3 per cent and 5 per cent of the workers attending the theatre. The workers of Nowa Huta, although generally of lower educational standard than Cracow workers, generally came from rural areas. Because of this they had none of the negative notions of the theatre as a place for the better off and not one for working people, which had become established over generations among the working class of Cracow. The point, however, is not so much that Nowa Huta workers went, and Cracow workers didn't, but that Nowa Huta workers found no difficulty in appreciating and returning to see works which sometimes baffle audiences of the world's well-to-do intellectuals. A static socialization theory cannot allow for such dramatic realizations of potential, since nothing has been 'put in' by society which would make them possible.

Piaget's terminology might have been used in the very fine study of the development of group consciousness by Worsley, *The Trumpet Shall Sound* (1957b). Worsley was interested in the explanation of the strange phenomena of the New Guinea islands known as the Cargo Cults. In these messianic cults, religious leaders would emerge in various tribes, preaching the end of the existing world and the arrival of a great ship or aeroplane, which would provide all believers with an abundance of the necessaries of life. Believers often ceased work and destroyed their existing goods in expectation of the arrival of the Cargo. Worsley was able to show that this apparently irrational behaviour resulted from the assimilation of new and important events to an existing social consciousness. For the coming of white men had an immense impact in the technologically very undeveloped communities. The local inhabitants observed that the white men had tremendous power, and great wealth; their religion preached the coming end of the world (many fundamentalist Christian missions were established). But they never seemed to *work*. Since their wealth came in ships, or inland sometimes by plane, the secret of their wealth and power must lie in the Cargo. He who could procure the mystical secret of the Cargo, by which wealth appeared without having to be created by work, was the great prophet and leader. Thus the people's consciousness was also accommodated to the incorporation of new symbols, and the adoption of elements of Christian belief. But the situation was not stable. Not only did the Cargo never come when it 'should' have, but, since Cargo cult believers did not work, the cults aroused white opposition. Attempts to suppress them were interpreted by local inhabitants as attempts to deny the secret to blacks, and some of the cults began to turn into uprisings. Worsley carefully details the constant development of events by which the local people gradually began to 'demystify' their consciousness of the situation, so that the cult movements in some cases became transformed into non-religious nationalist movements. This example indicates how group social consciousness can develop under pressure of events, but develops in ways which can only be understood by an examination of the process of interactions starting from the previous consciousness of the participants. But can we go further than this; is there any way of measuring the social consciousness of the participants, of evaluating it? Worsley correctly rejects Weber's propositions that social actions can be categorized on an abstract basis into different types, but his whole analysis is informed by a structuralist conception of the framework within which events took place, which does not depend solely on the social consciousness of the participants (Worsley, 1957b, Appendix).

False consciousness

Here then is another very important reason for rejecting an approach which requires us to consider only the perceptions of the participants in a situation. It gives us no independent criterion by which to examine the perceptions. Anthropological studies, as we have shown in previous chapters, are impossible without such a criterion. There is nothing special about studies of less complex societies which makes the principles for their study inapplicable in studies of our own societies. Merton discusses rain ceremonials among the Hopi Indians, for example (Merton, 1964). The participants undoubtedly believe that they bring rain. Meteorologists tell us that they do not. If we have no way of going beyond the consciousness of the participants, the matter ends there; similarly with the succession ritual of the Ankole, and so on. Merton used the terms manifest and latent function to distinguish between what the Hopi *said* was the purpose of their rain ceremonials, and what was their explanation in terms of the structure, and we replaced the term function by the term explanation. It is also justifiable to describe the manifest explanation given by the Hopi of their ceremonial as a form of *false consciousness*. This is not to say that it is illogical in terms of the belief systems and customs of the Hopi. Anthropologists have shown us very clearly the internal logicality of magical beliefs and the methods of their reinforcement (e.g. Evans-Pritchard, 1937). Rather, it is to say that

(a) it doesn't produce the intended results, and

(b) that an alternative explanation in terms of structure is more satisfactory.

A brief discussion of the notion of false consciousness is contained in Willer and Zollschan's otherwise arid article on revolutions in (Zollschan and Hirsch, 1964, p. 132). The idea of false consciousness presents no theoretical problems in a structuralist sociology. The major theoretical problem lies in the clear identification of structural conditions and conflicts in a complex social structure. Only when this has been done are we able to categorize the consciousness of a group in relation to the social structure. What happens if we try to apply the idea of false consciousness to conflict situations between groups?

Let us revert to a model of a simple social structure in which there are only two groups, similar to that introduced on page 72. In social structure B, groups x and y are in a potential conflict relationship, as a result of group x's structural superiority. In the actual historical experience of group y, therefore, this will mean that group y's structural position will continually induce situations in which dissatisfaction is felt. It is in group y's interests to change the structure, but not in group x's. Remembering that social consciousness is always an intervening variable in explaining a social situation, anything that deflects the consciousness of members of group y from a realization of their position of structural inferiority will be advantageous to group x, as will anything that justifies group x's position to members of that group. Speaking metaphorically, we can say that the structural conflict is reflected in the social consciousness of groups x and y. The following types of false consciousness might develop, singly or in combination.

1. The *ritualization* of the problem by a procedure such as that described earlier among the Zulu, when women took men's clothes, etc., for a day (p. 44), or the period of the Bairu mock kingship among the Ankole (p. 47). Such a safety valve facilitates the deflection of social consciousness from the structural problem.

2. Pressures on the participants to believe that the problem results from another cause than the real structural one. For example, studies of unemployment in the depression revealed that unemployed workers came to feel that their own personal inadequacies were responsible for their unemployment, rather than the breakdown of the capitalist economic system, their structural cause (Bakke, 1940). The acceptance of this type of substitution we may term *alienation*. There is one very important variant of this type of false consciousness. If participants can be made to believe that a sub group, z, usually part of y, is the real cause of the problem, the real structural cause is overlooked. Thus, the Jews became blamed for the crises in German society after world war one (Neumann, 1966). White and black workers are set against each other on grounds of colour (U.S.A.) (Cox, 1959); Protestant and Catholic workers are set against each other on grounds of religion (N. Ireland) (Gibbon, 1969).

3. Pressures on the participants to believe that the situation is inevitable, 'god given', unalterable, a 'natural', 'right', or 'correct' state. For instance, studies of political views in Britain have shown that there are many 'deference voters'—working class people who vote Tory because they have come to believe that the Conservative elite has a natural right to rule (McKenzie and Silver, 1968). Similarly, some women have accepted as natural their subordinate social and economic position. Viola Klein, in her study of working women, reports: 'There

is no trace of feminist egalitarianism—militant or otherwise—in any of the women's answers to our questionnaire, nor is it even implicitly assumed that women have a "right to work".' (Klein, 1960, cited in Mitchell, 1966.) This type of false consciousness may be termed *mystification*.

4. Pressures to believe that the consequences of changes will be worse than the existing state—for instance, the symbolic execution of the Bairu mock king, or De Gaulle's presentation of political alternatives to the French electorate in various referenda during the 1960s, or constant harping on fear of the 'unknown', or the presentation of unfortunate experiences of other peoples in different structural circumstances as if they were the inevitable consequence of any change.

5. Pressures which induce groups to evaluate their existing state positively in comparison with either the conditions of other groups, or with their own previous experiences, thus deflecting their attention from their structurally inferior position. For instance, Runciman has carried out a study which examined inequalities with regard to wealth, status and power between working and middle class groups in the period between 1918 and 1962 (Runciman, 1966). Finding big differences persisting, he examined the *attitudes* of samples of different social classes, both from written statements and from questionnaires. The responses indicated that the groups and individuals to which the respondents referred in considering their position in relation to the three criteria, were those close to them socially. They saw their position as being a little better or a little worse off than that of their social neighbours, rather than considering their position in relation to the whole social structure. Runciman's work is spoiled because it lacks a concept of social structure, which leads him into mistakes in his definitions of class, an inability to

explain the persistence of inequality, an inadequate framework for the explanation of why people judge as they do, and which is partially responsible for a totally misconceived attempt to find a non-social means of measuring social justice and injustice at the end. Nevertheless, it remains one of the most stimulating studies carried out in British sociology in recent years.

We must amplify the model somewhat. Suppose, firstly, that group x maintained its superiority over group y by force—coercion alone; its members may come to believe any of the different types of explanation for their superiority, but members of group y will not. In this case, group x's beliefs are a justification or rationalization of their superior structural position. We may call them an *ideology* (c.f., Mannheim, 1960).

Suppose, secondly, that a considerable number of members of group y come to believe that elements of group x's ideology are true. They internalize the norms of the dominant group—to use jargon. The ideology thus becomes a dominant one. This will be made easier if group x controls the information system.

Suppose, thirdly, that all, or almost all of the members of group y accept the ideology of group x, have internalized x's norms. In this case, group x will have an ideological *hegemony*.

It follows from this that the more the situation nears hegemony, the less coercion will be required to maintain the status quo. In the explanation of the continuance of the structural dominance of group x over group y, the coercion factor will be decreased in importance as we move from the first to the third situation. It is very difficult for a group to maintain dominance over another group for a long period by coercion alone. Rousseau once expressed the same thought: 'However strong a man is, he is never sufficiently strong to remain a master for ever, unless his power is transformed into Right, Obedi-

ence and Duty.' The degree of ideology, ideological dominance, ideological hegemony in a social situation has to
be investigated by the sociologist. For instance, Marcuse
has tried to argue in his book, *One Dimensional Man*,
that the United States remains riven with structural conflict, but that a major deprived group, the white working class, has so internalized the norms of the dominant
group, the industrial controllers, that their potential as
agents of change has almost been eliminated, and that
smaller groups, especially Black American workers, whose
deprivation is more extreme, and who are excluded by
definition from the ideological hegemony—since it is racist
in conception—will act as agents of change, initially at
any rate.

We are in no way trying to say that any of the various
kinds of false consciousness which may manifest themselves in different social situations are necessarily consciously thought out attempts to justify or to delude a
subordinate group by a dominant one. To reiterate a
constant theme, sometimes they may be, sometimes they
may partially be, sometimes they may develop out of
the continuance of a situation, and may transform the
means by which its continuance is maintained—a situation based on coercion may be transformed into one of
acceptance. However, strains and tensions arising from
the structurally inferior position of a group itself continue to occur, even if the social consciousness of the
group is itself deflected so that no attempts to change the
situation are made. In such cases, frustrations arising
from structural deprivations may be *displaced*, to adopt
a Freudian term, from their real structural cause on to
other objects or activities. Such displacement may occur
in coercion situations also, where people who are conscious of the basis of their problems can do nothing about
it. There is, for instance, a tremendously high rate of
theft from factories in Eastern Europe, where strikes are

forbidden, and a considerable amount of industrial sabotage in Britain too (e.g., Cliff, 1964, ch. 14). Where the problem is not simply powerlessness in the face of coercion, but false consciousness, the behaviour may seem initially to be irrational, or senselessly violent. This kind of situation provides one basis for structural theories of delinquency, and to some extent, 'deviancy' in general (Taylor and Taylor, 1968). To the extent that this is true, the removal of false consciousness in such situations will affect the displaced behaviour as well.

In this chapter, we have tried to dispute approaches which ignore or pay only lip service to the ways in which people see the society in which they live; and also to challenge approaches which tend to view sociology in these terms alone. As an alternative we have argued that the general approach for examining relations between structure and social consciousness should be that of a process of interaction in which structure is dominant— a structured dialectic. By a critical examination of ways sociologists view the process by which an individual's social consciousness develops—his socialization—in which, as usual, we have attacked static, one-way approaches, we have been led to a classification of key processes by which social consciousness may be distorted in situations of conflict relations between groups. It may be noticed that, while in the last chapter our emphasis was on social change, we proposed that our arguments were applicable to all situations. In the latter part of this chapter, we have emphasized factors by which change is retarded, yet, once again, this approach can be applied to all social situations, not just those when change does not occur.

6

Conclusion

The need for a critical approach

In this short book we have not tried to give long lists of facts about 'the family in Britain'; or the percentage of working class children who enter university. Such facts are in some degree available if you wish to find them. On the contrary, we have been interested in the explanation of such things, the 'why' questions, the move from description to understanding, the reasons for finding out one set of facts rather than another. As this is an introductory book, we are therefore inviting students to ask the same questions of their teachers and courses. *Why* are you being taught in this or that way? This problem has two kinds of answer.

1. In the main part of the book, we have attempted to provide the basis of an answer by an examination of some of the common orientations to sociology, reserving our strongest criticism for the misconception that there is some built-in tendency to order which societies 'have', a misconception which we have challenged on both theoretical and practical grounds. It is important to attack this misconception because it is so common in various forms, especially in British and American sociology. It is a misconception which distorts reality, diverts

attention from the main problems, devalues history, and provides a terminology and approach which dehumanizes man in the interests of a crude and fallacious determinism.

In making these main attacks, we have levelled criticisms at some other approaches—the mirror image of functionalism which substitutes change for order, and views which tend to elevate social consciousness as if it were the only permissible focus of attention. We have also presented the outlines of an alternative approach, which we consider to indicate the way social reality can be scientifically studied by sociologists. This approach does not come 'out of our heads', but from reading and research. If a rough label is required, it may be called historical structuralism, or dynamic structuralism, in that it makes no assumptions about any forms of inbuilt purposes of societies (a semantic error), but demands that, for the explanation of why a society exhibits change X, order Y, or its population behaviour Z, and for predicting how such phenomena will develop in the future, it is essential to study the process of interactions by which the structural factors involved have developed—to use a dialectical method.

2. As well as trying to demonstrate the fallacies of the approaches criticized, it is necessary also to examine *why* these fallacies have such power; this is a sociological problem, and by examining it in the first chapter we hope to have shown not only something of the basis of the problems you as students face, but also in doing so to have introduced sociological methods of analysis.

If part of the explanation of why sociologists do things the way they do lies in an examination of the structural position of sociologists, and is thus a necessary part of the investigation, similarly, part of the explanation of why all of us do the things we do lies in an examination of our own structural positions; in engaging in self-analysis of this type we are undertaking sociological introspection. If the reasons for our actions are not clear to us, or if they are in fact other than we believe them to be, we cannot be said to be able to choose to act, to be responsible for our actions. It is our view that sociology is potentially a humanistic discipline in that it can increase the area of choice men have over their actions. It can enable them to locate the sources to which they must go if they wish to change things, and the necessary means, thus providing man with a potential scientific basis for action, increasing him, rather than cramping him into a straight jacket of determinism provided by explanations in terms of how he 'fits in' to the social order (Ossowski, 1962).

Objectivity and controversy

Although the subject matter of sociology is real—the behaviour of people in societies over time—there are insurmountable problems in providing a non-controversial, objective science of sociology. A fundamental difference exists between the study of natural objects and that of man. Stone is in no way affected by a geologist's analysis of the geological strata of which it forms a part, but human groups may be profoundly affected by a sociological study, since social consciousness, an intervening variable, may be changed by it. Thus, publication of a sociological analysis, even if objective, may be a political act. Publication in Ankole of an objective analysis of the structural basis of the inferiority of the Bairu in relation to the Bahima would almost certainly have lost the author his head.

Suppose it were objectively the case that a complex social structure, like ours, was based on the exploitation and manipulation of some groups in the interests of others, and that a sociologist published an objectively true account of how this developed and persisted, using, we should like to hope, the means we have outlined in the book. This publication could affect social consciousness; it would tend to decrease false consciousness, possibly making subordinate groups more dissatisfied with their position, arousing the conscience of some of those in the superior groups. Even if it did not actually do this to any great extent, it might be felt by some that it would be likely to have such an effect.

Certainly, replies to the objective analysis could be expected; written with erudition and intelligence, they would attempt to show that the analysis was not objective, but distorted. The writers of such reactions would not only be wrong, but knaves—distorting science for political ends; they might, however, persuade people.

Other writers, realizing that their career advancement and security could be promoted by not offending dominant groups, might put forward arguments that deflected attention from the analysis—that the job of sociology should be to study something else, like how social order is maintained, perhaps—or that sociology does not have the technique to study major problems, and should therefore confine itself to areas where available techniques could be used—studies of opinions about sport, or of how people spend their time, and so on. Objectivity means technique, they might say. How can your study be objective, since you do not use multiple regression analysis, which is really so sophisticated? Such people would not only be wrong, but cowards.

In our hypothetical example, we see the true scientist beset by knaves and cowards confusing the issue, distorting the student's mind from the real truth.

But in the reality of our own societies, how do we distinguish between the true sociologist, the knave and the coward? In the hypothetical case, we presumed to know which was the objective analysis. In our own society, how do we know who is objective, who knave and who coward? The very labels depend on our knowing this, and we do not. We are left with the controversies which characterize sociology today; as to how to judge them— our views on that have been the subject of the book. One of the reasons, apart from simplicity, that we have made use of examples from anthropology is that it does not greatly affect *us* that, for instance, the Bahima exploited the Bairu; therefore we could make our point about structural conflict in a not too controversial way. If the point has been well made, apply it to the analysis of our own society, but do not expect your analysis to be non-controversial, even if you are convinced that it is the most scientific available.

Values and involvement

The study of stones does not raise moral problems in itself; it is nonsensical to ask—should a stone be carboniferous or calcic? Moral problems derive from the human situation—it *is* meaningful to ask—should a social group be in a structurally inferior position to another group? Thus the actual subject matter of sociology is the basis of moral judgments.

In our hypothetical case, we have used value laden terms—knave and coward—and had to discard them. But in the sociologist's real work, he faces moral dilemmas. Is his purpose in undertaking a study objective, or is his choice subject to social pressures of the kinds we have described? This is itself a legitimate sociological problem. If he studies X (say, fashions in dress), rather than Y (say, the power structure of a society), when on the answers to Y the well-being of humanity might depend, may he not be morally guilty, and may his justifications of his decision not be rationalizations?

Furthermore, he also has been, and is being, socialized as a human being, as part of a society. Is he not likely to have views and opinions, assumptions and prejudices of a non-scientific nature, and are these not likely to intrude, both in his selection of topics, and in the way he investigates them?—we are again back to chapter 1. Many sociologists, in spite of heavy and constant attacks from writers like Lynd (1939), Myrdal (1962), Gouldner (1963), Seeley (1963), ignore such problems in the name of trying to establish a 'science'; as if a study were made more scientific by ignoring problems. If real problems exist which cannot be examined by a particular technique, then to ignore them means that to be more 'scientific' is to be less scientific.

Finally, as a human being, has the sociologist no concern for the world that is to be? Is it to develop towards the brutal totalitarian repression of 1984 (Orwell, 1965); or the smooth totalitarian manipulation of *Brave New World* (Huxley, 1958); or to stay forever as now (an impossibility, really); or to become a place where 'the free development of each is a condition of the free development of all.' (Marx.) Since the sociologist's research may be relevant in influencing what comes to be, has he not a moral choice to make, and may he not be judged by others on the basis of this choice? We would wish to argue that the greatest problem of sociology is the investigation of forms of social organization which do not limit, but widen the possibility of meaningful individual choice, and widen the horizons of people, so that decisions can be made not outside them, by forces which control them, but so that they are themselves in a position to decide as to their actions. Far from a society thus organized being an unchanging, conflictless utopia, only, as Marx argued, in such a society can *human* history be said to have begun (Bottomore and Rubel, 1963, part 5).

Our general point is, then, that, while social reality is objective, and the study of it theoretically may be objective, to claim that a non-controversial, value-free sociology can develop in a conflict-based social structure is theoretically untenable, practically unrealistic, and morally disastrous.

Methods and problems

One of the key points of emphasis in the book has been the necessity for dialectical analysis, which we have consistently defined as the study of processes of interaction. Historical structuralism implies dialectical approaches.

Many though not all of the mathematical tools which, for various reasons, have become popular among sociologists, particularly in America, are not suited to analysis of processes of interactions. Some are unsuitable for holistic analysis; a considerable number are static—that is, they depend on 'freezing' social reality at a particular moment, and then predicting by assuming that the relations between factors measured are constant over time. The grounds for this assumption are hardly ever spelled out, and it is therefore unscientific. In theory, therefore, the whole scientific basis of the work disappears. Only after an examination of the problem dialectically can we make assumptions about the constancy of relations examined at a given time. This indicates another reason for the popularity of theories that assume social order to be society's basic state, since they allow the use of simple statistical techniques.

We do not by any means oppose the use of mathematics in sociology; but we do say that the methodological requirements of our subject are prior to the mathematics of it—the latter is a tool, and mathematicians must devise tools capable of being meaningfully applied to dialectical analysis, a very necessary task, as much historically based analysis is deficient in terms of techniques.

In many cases, sociologists, especially those with mathematical training, have become so mesmerized by the apparent quantifiability provided by their methods that they have argued that 'scientific' sociology only exists when such techniques are applied, and that only those problems should be studied where they do apply. The mathematical techniques have come to determine the subject matter (c.f., Blau and Duncan, 1967, reviewed by Riddell, 1968b). Of course, quantification makes a subject seem respectable. It sounds good to be able to say that 90 per cent of people think this or that at a probability level of .05—until we remember that unless we understand the dialectic of social structure and social consciousness which led them to express the opinion, we haven't really a clue about how they will think or behave tomorrow, or the day after. If, to take an example used by Barrington Moore, we study the incidence of reported male sexual aggressiveness on an American college campus, our study will be more amenable to statistical technique than if we study the origins and development of, say, the Vietnam war, or the development of the power structure of the Soviet Union (Moore, 1963). But that is no reason whatever for studying the former rather than the latter, and distorts sociology if it leads us to do so. The student of sociology should be especially wary of 'scientism'.

Some sociologists argue that a science can only be developed by amassing small bits of information, out of which theories will emerge—as if we did not have to make choices as to which bits of information to amass; while others propose that, by developing a theory of society in the abstract first, we shall be able to explain all the subordinate parts—as if the correct principles of such a general theory were floating in the abstract, to be absorbed by the perceptive mind, and only had to be put together. C. W. Mills has exposed these fallacies, which he calls 'abstracted empiricism' and 'grand theory', respectively, in a masterly way in his book *The Sociological*

Imagination (1959a). What these views have in common
is that they lead away from the study of social structures
in historical development, the one by never considering
the whole, the other by never carrying out any study. The
relationship between theory and empirical research is of
a dialectical nature. In the process of testing by empirical
research ideas derived from common experience or previous study, theories are developed which are refined, modified in application, and so on—subject to the sorts of
distortion we have talked about at the beginning of this
book. However, if the central focus of sociology is structuralism, and yet few structural studies are carried out, we
need not be surprised at the number of poor sociological
theories that are around.

Abstracted empiricism has been closely connected with
static mathematical techniques, and grand theory with the
multiplication of new terms, which we have argued earlier
often parallel the complexity of reality rather than explaining it. All sociologists and prospective sociologists, then,
should firmly keep in mind that the equation:

Scientific Technique + Jargon = Science

does not necessarily hold.

The offshore island

As we write, the state of sociology in Britain is not such
that the student will find he is generally confronted by
intellects of the calibre of Parsons or Mills, Levi-Strauss or
Althusser, Marcuse or Habermass, Ossowski or Hochfeld,
Markovic or Supek. As Perry Anderson has observed, it is
redolent of the quality of British culture that no great
indigenous schools of sociology have developed (Anderson,
1968).

Sociology in Britain has developed rapidly in recent
years; career advancement has been very easy, and many
sociologists have quickly found it congenial to become ad-

ministrators and organizers of departments. The critical student will find that much of the work is poor in conceptualization, abounds in logical errors, substitutes description for explanation, and assumes the answers to problems it should examine. Much of the research has been narrowly empiricist, based on a 'let's put all the data in the computer—something significant is bound to come out' approach, and, while functionalism has not the overwhelming predominance it has had in the United States—although we have some of the naïvest functionalists in the game, especially in educational sociology (e.g., Musgrave, 1965, Shipman, 1968), and it appears to be increasing in importance, there is often to be found a mild iconoclasm, part liberal, part fabian in heritage, which substitutes for a theoretical analysis. Names such as Bottomore, Lockwood and Rex indicate exceptions to this, as does much of the work associated with the political journal *New Left Review*; some examples are indicated in the next section.

We hope that reading this book will help to stimulate you to evaluate your course sociologically; to investigate how the controversies discussed here are presented to you, and whether they are adequately met; what principles are used in selecting facts for presentation to you; what sorts of problems are included in your studies, and why. We are satisfied if you have been provided with some basis to challenge your teachers, and encouraged to develop a critical attitude to all that you are taught. To refute them will, we hope, usually require wider study—some leads can be found in the suggestions for further reading and in the bibliography.

Suggestions for further reading

Suggestions for further reading

A fairly wide selection of references to the work of sociologists with different approaches has been given in the text and they are detailed in the bibliography. These suggestions are *not* meant as a comprehensive book list, but as an indication of some of the writings from which our perspective has developed. They are divided into general and theoretical studies, and studies of specific problems.

General studies and theoretical origins

In Britain, the major, perhaps the only significant general sociologist is Bottomore. His *Sociology* (1963), though some students find it dull, has no rival in the English language, and his studies *Elites in Society* (1967) and *Classes in Modern Society* (1966) are thoughtful introductions. In addition, his translations with Rubel of Marx indicate how much maligned that great sociologist has been (Karl Marx, *Selected Writings*, 1963). A figure of equivalent stature in America, though of quite different personality and style, was C. Wright Mills. His attacks on prevailing orthodoxy, and advocacy of structuralist sociology are made in *The Sociological Imagination* (1959a) and in his collected essays,

Power, Politics and People (edited by I. Horowitz, 1963).
Both his *Images of Man* (1967) and *The Marxists* (1963)
are major attempts to break down parochialism, while
Character and Social Structure (Gerth and Mills, 1954)
remains, in spite of many mistakes, a landmark in attempts
to integrate sociology and social psychology. His influence
can also be felt in the important critical selection edited by
Stein and Vidich, *Sociology on Trial* (1963).

In theoretical terms, we have referred to Althusser as
a major writer, and would particularly refer to his article,
Contradiction and Overdetermination (1967). A more detailed examination of the origins of dialectics is provided
by Marcuse in *Reason and Revolution* (1968), and a more
conventional approach to conflict sociology by John Rex,
another British sociologist of note, in *Key Problems of
Sociological Theory* (1963). Finally, two books which we
consider of great importance in understanding theoretical
backgrounds, and which are not too difficult, are V. Venable's *Human Nature* (1966), and E. Mandel's *Marxist
Economic Theory, Vols. 1 and 2* perhaps the greatest work
of Marxist scholarship in recent times, and as much
sociology as economics (1968a).

Critiques

It is very useful to be aware of some critiques of commonly
held viewpoints, so as to assist in their refutation—here is
a small selection. Several of the works already referred to
already contain critiques; in addition R. Lynd's old study
Knowledge for What (1939) is still as relevant as ever.
I. Horowitz examines one aspect of the involvement of
government in sociology in *The Rise and Fall of Project
Camelot* (1967), as does K. Gough in more general terms in
Anthropology and Imperialism (1968). A very clear and
concise criticism of functionalism by M. Pečuljić a Yugoslav sociologist, will appear in a volume of translations

from Yugoslav sociology now in preparation (*Functionalism. Basic Ideas and Critique*, 1965). Several critiques of Parsonian functionalism have been listed on page 38, and articles by Orlansky (1949) and Lindesmith and Strauss (1950) deal with the culture-personality school. Finally, Cicourel's *Method and Measurement in Sociology* (1964) examines with a critical eye methods in common use.

Particular studies

It is only by examination in relation to actual problems that any sociological approach can be evaluated. Here are just a few examples from different areas. For highly complex societies, try R. Miliband, *The State in Capitalist Society* (1969), P. Anderson, *The Origins of the Present Crisis* (1964) (Britain); C. W. Mills, *The Power Elite* (1957), P. Baran and M. Sweezy, *Monopoly Capital* (1968) (America); I. Deutscher, *The Unfinished Revolution* (1967) (Soviet Union). For countries suffering from underdevelopment, try two articles and a book by A. G. Frank (1966, 1967a, 1967b), Pierre Jalee's *The Pillage of the Third World* (1968) and P. Baran's *The Political Economy of Growth* (1967). Two notable specific examples of analysis are P. Anderson, *Portugal and the End of Ultra Colonialism* (1962), R. Blackburn, *Prologue to the Cuban Revolution* (1963).

O. C. Cox disentangles problems of race in his major work, *Caste, Class and Race* (1959). Examples of notable studies of social consciousness are S. Ossowski, *Class Structure in the Social Consciousness* (1963), P. Worsley, *The Trumpet Shall Sound* (1957b), and William Hinton's magnificent account of the transformation of a Chinese village, *Fanshen* (1968). Finally, two examples of studies of social groups within our society: David Lockwood's examination of the changing middle class, *Blackcoated Worker* (1958), and the study of a mining community by Dennis et. al., *Coal Is Our Life* (1956).

Journals

It is important to look through the sociological journals to examine what sort of things are being done, what sort of trends are making headway. But in terms of historical structuralist sociology, the best journal in Britain is undoubtedly *New Left Review*; in America, *Monthly Review* and *Science and Society*. Much more appears in European journals, but there is a language problem. However, *Polish Sociological Bulletin* appears in English and contains much interesting material (or has done—at the time of writing many Polish sociologists have been dismissed or imprisoned for their work), and there is the international edition of *Praxis* from Yugoslavia. Perhaps more people can cope with French; there are many excellent journals, of which the new *L'Homme et la Société* is of particular note. One of the major points we have been trying to make is the need to avoid the parochialism which makes it easy for a sociology teacher to put over a particular 'line' without question. Such journals, among others, should be in every library, with back numbers. Are they in yours?

Bibliography

ALLEN, V. (1966), *Militant Trade Unionism*, London, Merlin Press.

ALTHUSSER, L. (1967), 'Contradiction and Overdetermination', *New Left Review*, no. 41, pp. 11-35.

ANDERSON, P. (1962), 'Portugal and the End of Ultra Colonialism', *New Left Review*, no. 15, pp. 83-102, no. 16, pp. 88-123, and no. 17, pp. 85-114.

ANDERSON, P. (1964), 'The Origins of the Present Crisis', *New Left Review*, no. 23, pp. 26-54.

ANDERSON, P. (1968), 'Components of the National Culture', *New Left Review*, no. 50, pp. 3-57.

ARON, R. (1968), *Main Currents of Sociological Thought*, Vol. 1, Harmondsworth, Penguin.

BAKKE, E. (1940), *The Unemployed Worker*, Yale, Yale University Press.

BANTON, M. (1965), *Roles*, London, Tavistock.

BARAN, P. (1967), *The Political Economy of Growth*, London, Monthly Review Press.

BARAN, P. & SWEEZY, P. (1968), *Monopoly Capital*, Harmondsworth, Penguin.

BARNES, H., editor, (1961), *An Introduction to the History of Sociology*, Chicago, University of Chicago Press.

BARRATT-BROWN, M. (1963), *After Imperialism*, London,

Heinemann.

BECKER, H., editor, (1964), *The Other Side*, London, Collier-Macmillan.

BENEDICT, R. (1912), *Patterns of Culture*, London, Routledge & Kegan Paul.

BENOIT-SMULLYAN, E. (1961), *The Sociologism of Emile Durkheim and His School*, in Barnes (1961), q.v.

BERGER, P. (1963), *Invitation to Sociology*, Harmondsworth, Penguin.

BERGER, P. & PULLBERG, S. (1966), 'Reification and the Sociological Critique of Consciousness', *New Left Review*, no. 35, pp. 56-71.

BETTLEHEIM, B. (1943), 'Individual and Mass Behaviour in Extreme Situations', *Journal of Abnormal and Social Psychology*, pp. 417-452.

BIDDLE, B. & THOMAS, E. (1966), *Role Theory: Concepts and Research*, New York, Wiley.

BIRNBAUM, N. (1958), 'Social Constraints and Academic Freedom', *Universities and Left Review*, no. 5, pp. 47-52.

BLACK, M., editor, (1961), *The Sociological Theories of Talcott Parsons*, Englewood Cliffs, N.J., Prentice Hall.

BLACKBURN, R. (1963), 'Prologue to the Cuban Revolution', *New Left Review*, no. 21, pp. 52-91.

BLACKBURN, R. (1967), *The Unequal Society*, in Blackburn & Cockburn (1967), q.v.

BLACKBURN, R. (1969), *A Brief Guide to Bourgeois Ideology*, in Cockburn & Blackburn (1969), q.v.

BLACKBURN, R. & COCKBURN, A., editors, (1967), *The Incompatibles*, Harmondsworth, Penguin.

BLAU, P. & DUNCAN, O. (1967), *The American Occupational Structure*, London, Wiley.

BLUMBERG, P. (1968), *Industrial Democracy: The Sociology of Participation*, London, Constable.

BOTTOMORE, T. (1963), *Sociology*, London, Unwin University Books.

BOTTOMORE, T. (1966), *Classes in Modern Society*, London, George Allen & Unwin.

BOTTOMORE, T. (1967a), *Elites and Society*, Harmondsworth, Penguin.

BOTTOMORE, T. (1967b), *Critics of Society*, London, George Allen & Unwin.

BOTTOMORE, T. & RUBEL, M., editors, (1963), *Karl Marx, Selected Writings*, Harmondsworth, Penguin.

BROOM, L. & SELZNICK, P. (1963), *Sociology*, New York, Harper & Row.

CAPLOW, T. & MCGHEE, R. (1961), *The Academic Market-place*, New York, Science Editions.

CARMICHAEL, S. (1968), *Black Power—Address To Congress*, London, Institute of Phenomenological Studies, Long playing record, D.L.6.

CARR, E. (1966), *The Bolshevik Revolution, 1917-1923. Vol. 1*, Harmondsworth, Penguin.

CHINOY, E. (1967), *Society*, New York, Random House.

CICOUREL, A. (1964), *Method and Measurement in Sociology*, London, Collier-Macmillan.

CLIFF, T. (1964), *Russia—A Marxist Analysis*, London, International Socialism.

COCKBURN, A. & BLACKBURN, R., editors, (1969), *Student Power*, Harmondsworth, Penguin.

COHEN, P. (1968), *Modern Social Theory*, London, Heinemann.

COHN-BENDIT, D. *et al.* (1969), *Why Sociologists?*, in Cockburn & Blackburn (1969), q.v.

COSER, L. & ROSENBERG, B., editors, (1964), *Sociological Theory*, London, Collier-Macmillan.

COTGROVE, S. (1967), *The Science of Society*, London, Heinemann.

COULSON, M. *et. al.* (1967), 'Towards A Sociological Theory of Occupational Choice—A Critique', *Sociological Review*, Vol. 15(3), pp. 301-309.

COX, O. (1959), *Caste, Class and Race*, New York, Monthly Review Press.

DAHRENDORF, R. (1964), *Out of Utopia*, in Coser & Rosenberg (1964), q.v.

DENNIS, N. *et. al.* (1956), *Coal Is Our Life*, London, Eyre & Spottiswoode.

DEUTSCHER, I. (1967), *The Unfinished Revolution*, London, Oxford University Press.

DURKHEIM, E. (1952), *Suicide*, London, Routledge & Kegan Paul.

ELIAS, N. (1956), 'Problems of Involvement and Detachment', *British Journal of Sociology*, Vol. VII, p. 226f.

ENGELS, F. (1958), *Karl Marx, A Contribution to the Critique of Political Economy*, in Marx, K. and Engels (1958), q.v.

ENGELS, F. (1958), *Ludwig Feuerbach and the End of Classical German Philosophy*, in Marx and Engels (1958), q.v.

EVANS-PRITCHARD, E. (1937), *Witchcraft, Oracles and Magic Among the Azande*, Oxford, Clarendon Press.

FIAMENGO, A. (1967), *Osnove Opće Sociologije*, Zagreb, Narodne Novine.

FORTES, M. & EVANS-PRITCHARD, E., editors, (1961), *African Political Systems*, London, Oxford University Press.

FOSS, D. (1963), 'The World View of Talcott Parsons', in Stein & Vidich (1963), q.v.

FRANK, A. (1966), 'The Development of Underdevelopment', *Monthly Review*, Vol. 18(4), pp. 17-31.

FRANK, A. (1967a), *Capitalism and Underdevelopment in Latin America*, London, Monthly Review Press.

FRANK, A. (1967b), 'The Sociology of Development and the Underdevelopment of Sociology', *Catalyst*, no. 3, pp. 20-73.

FRANKENBERG, R. (1967), *Communities in Britain*, Harmondsworth, Penguin.

GERTH, H. & MILLS, C. (1954), *Character and Social Structure*, London, Routledge & Kegan Paul.

GIBBON, P. (1969), 'The Dialectic of Religion and Class in Ulster', *New Left Review*, no. 55, pp. 20-41.

GIDDENS, A. (1965), 'The Suicide Problem in French Sociology', *British Journal of Sociology*, Vol. XVI(1), pp. 3-18.

GIDDENS, A. (1966), 'A Typology of Suicide', *European Journal of Sociology*, Vol. 7(2), pp. 276-95.

GIDDENS, A. (1968), 'Power in the Recent Writings of Talcott Parsons', *Sociology*, Vol. II(3), pp. 257-72.

GLUCKMAN, M. (1944), *Malinowski's Sociological Theories*, London, Oxford University Press.

GLUCKMAN, M. (1955), *Custom and Conflict in Africa*, Oxford, Blackwell.

GODELIER, M. (1967), *System, Structure and Contradiction in Capital*, in Miliband and Saville (1967), q.v.

GOFFMAN, E. (1959), *The Presentation of Self in Everyday Life*, New York, Doubleday Anchor.

GOFFMAN, E. (1968), *Asylums*, Harmondsworth, Penguin.

GOFFMAN, E. (1969), *Where the Action Is*, London, Allen Lane, The Penguin Press.

GOODE, W. (1964), *The Family*, Englewood Cliffs, N.J., Prentice Hall.

GORER, G. & RICKMAN, J. (1949), *The People of Great Russia*, London.

GOUGH, E. K. (1952), 'Changing Kinship Usages in the Setting of Political and Economic Change among the Nayars of Malabar', *Journal of the Royal Anthropological Institute of Great Britain and Ireland*, Vol. XXXII, pp. 71-87.

GOUGH, E. K. (1968), 'Anthropology and Imperialism', *Monthly Review*, Vol. 19(11), pp. 12-27.

GOULDNER, A. (1963), *Anti-Minotaur. The Myth of a Value Free Sociology*, in Stein and Vidich (1963), q.v.

GOULDTHORPE, J. & LOCKWOOD, D. (1963), 'Affluence and the British Class Structure', *Sociological Review*, Vol. II, pp. 133-63.

GROSS, L., editor, (1959), *Symposium on Sociological Theory*, Evanston, Row Peterson.

GROSS, N. *et al.* (1958), *Explorations in Role Analysis*, New York, Wiley.

HART, H. (1959), *Social Theory and Social Change*, in Gross (1959), q.v.

HINTON, W. (1968), *Fanshen*, London, Merlin Press.

HOROWITZ, I., editor (1963), *Power, Politics and People*, London, Oxford University Press.

HOROWITZ, I. (1967), *The Rise and Fall of Project Camelot*, Massachusetts, MIT Press.

HOROWITZ, I. (1968), *Professing Sociology*, Chicago, Aldine Pub. Co.

HORTON, P. & HUNT, C. (1964), *Sociology*, London, McGraw-Hill.

HOSELITZ, B. (1966), *Main Concepts in the Analysis of the Social Implications of Technical Change*, in Hoselitz & Moore (1966), q.v.

HOSELITZ, B. & MOORE, W., editors (1966), *Industrialization and Society*, U.N.E.S.C.O., Mouton.

HUXLEY, A. (1958), *Brave New World*, Harmondsworth, Penguin.

INKELES, A. (1964), *What Is Sociology?*, Englewood Cliffs, N.J., Prentice Hall.

JACKSON, B. & MARSDEN, D. (1962), *Education and the Working Class*, London, Routledge & Kegan Paul.

JALEE, P. (1968), *The Pillage of the Third World*, London, Monthly Review Press.

JOHNSTON, T. (1929), *A History of the Working Classes in Scotland*, Glasgow, Forward Publishing Co.

KARDINER, A., editor (1945), *Psychological Frontiers of Society*, New York, Columbia University Press.

KLEIN, V. (1960), *Working Wives*, London, Institute of Personnel Management Occasional Papers, no. 15.

LAZARSFELD, P. & THIELENS, W. (1955), *The Academic Mind*, Glencoe, Ill., Free Press.

LEFEBVRE, H. (1968), *The Sociology of Marx*, London, Allen Lane, The Penguin Press.

LERNER, D. (1964), *The Passing of Traditional Society*, London, Collier-Macmillan.

LESSNOFF, M. (1968), 'Parsons' System Problems', *Sociological Review*, Vol. 16(2), pp. 185-215.

LINDESMITH, A. & STRAUSS, A. (1950), 'A Critique of Culture-Personality Writings', *American Sociological Review*, Vol. 15, pp. 587-600.

LINTON, R. (1961), *The Cultural Background of Personality*, London, Routledge & Kegan Paul.

LIPSET, S. & SMELSER, N. (1961), 'Change and Controversy in Recent American Sociology', *British Journal of Sociology*, Vol. XII(2), pp. 41-51.

LOCKWOOD, D. (1958), *The Blackcoated Worker*, London, George Allen & Unwin.

LYND, R. (1939), *Knowledge for What?*, Princeton, Princeton University Press.

MCCLELLAND, D. (1961), *The Achieving Society*, Princeton, N.J., Van Nostrand.

MACINTOSH, M. (1968), 'The Homosexual Role', *Social Problems*, Vol. 16(2), pp. 182-92.

MACINTYRE, A. (1967), *A Short History of Ethics*, London, Routledge & Kegan Paul.

MACINTYRE, A. (1969), *New Trends in Sociological Theory*, paper given to B.S.A. Teachers' Section Conference, L.S.E., January, 1969.

MCKENZIE, R. & SILVER, A. (1968), *Angels in Marble*, London, Heinemann.

MALINOWSKI, B. (1922), *Argonauts of the Western Pacific*, London.

MALINOWSKI, B. (1944), *A Scientific Theory of Culture*, Chapel Hill, University of North Carolina Press.

MANDEL, E. (1968a), *Marxist Economic Theory*, Vols. 1 and 2, London, Merlin Press.

MANDEL, E. (1968b), 'The Lessons of May, 1968', *New Left Review*, no. 52, pp. 9-32.

MANNHEIM, K. (1960), *Ideology and Utopia*, London, Routledge & Kegan Paul.

MARCUSE, H. (1964), *One Dimensional Man*, London, Routledge & Kegan Paul.

MARCUSE, H. (1968a), *Reason and Revolution*, London, Routledge & Kegan Paul.

MARCUSE, H. (1968b), *Soviet Marxism*, London, Routledge & Kegan Paul.

MARX, K. (1958), *The Civil War in France* and *The 18th Brumaire of Louis Napoleon*, in Marx and Engels (1958), q.v.

MARX, K. & ENGELS, F. (1958), *Selected Works*, *Vols. 1 and 2*, London, Lawrence & Wishart.

MAYO, E. (1957), *The Social Problems of an Industrial Civilization*, London, Routledge & Kegan Paul.

MEAD, G. (1934), *Mind, Self and Society*, Chicago, University of Chicago Press.

MEAD, M. (1935), *Sex and Temperament in Three Primitive Societies*, London, Routledge & Kegan Paul.

MERRINGTON, J. (1968), *Theory and Practice in Gramsci's Marxism*, in Miliband & Saville (1968), q.v.

MERTON, R. (1964a), *The Role Set: Problems in Sociological Theory*, in Coser & Roseberg (1964), q.v.

MERTON, R. (1964b), *Social Theory and Social Structure*, London, Collier-Macmillan.

MILIBAND, R. (1969), *The State in Capitalist Society*, London, Weidenfeld & Nicholson.

MILIBAND, R. & SAVILLE, J., editors (1967), *Socialist Register*, *1967*, London, Merlin Press.

MILIBAND, R. & SAVILLE, J., editors (1968), *Socialist Register*, *1968*, London, Merlin Press.

MILL, J. (1866), *Auguste Comte and Positivism*, London, Trench Trubner.

MILLS, C. (1957), *The Power Elite*, New York, Oxford University Press.

MILLS, C. (1959a), *The Sociological Imagination*, New York, Oxford University Press.

MILLS, C. (1959b), *The Causes of World War III*, London, Secker & Warburg.

MILLS, C., editor, (1963), *The Marxists*, Harmondsworth, Penguin.

MILLS, C., editor, (1967), *Images of Man*, New York, George Braziller.

MITCHELL, J. (1966), 'Women, The Longest Revolution', *New Left Review*, no. 40, pp. 11-37.

MOORE, B. (1963), *Strategy in Social Science*, in Stein & Vidich (1963), q.v.

MUSGRAVE, P. (1965), *The Sociology of Education*, London, Methuen.

MUSGRAVE, P. (1967), 'Towards a Sociological Theory of Occupational Choice', *Sociological Review*, Vol. 15(1), pp. 33-46.

MUSGROVE, F. & TAYLOR, P. (1969), *Society and the Teacher's Role*, London, Routledge & Kegan Paul.

MYRDAL, G. (1962), *Value in Social Theory*, London, Routledge & Kegan Paul.

NADEL, S. (1965), *The Theory of Social Structure*, London, Cohen & West.

NEUMANN, F. (1966), *Behemoth—The Structure and Practice of National Socialism*, New York, Harper & Row.

NISBET, R. (1967), *The Sociological Tradition*, London, Heinemann.

NOVACK, G. (1968), 'Positivism and Marxism in Sociology', *International Socialist Review*, Vol. 29(4), pp. 27-37.

OBERG, K. (1961), *The Kingdom of Ankole in Uganda*, in Fortes & Evans-Pritchard (1961), q.v.

ORLANSKY, H. (1949), 'Infant Care and Personality', *Psychological Bulletin*, Vol. 46.

ORWELL, G. (1965), *Nineteen Eighty-Four*, Harmondsworth, Penguin.

OSSOWSKI, S. (1962), 'Empirical Sociology and Inner Experience', *Polish Sociological Bulletin*, Vol. 2(3-4), pp. 5-14.

OSSOWSKI, S. (1963), *Class Structure in the Social Consciousness*, London, Routledge & Kegan Paul.

PALLISTER, H. (1938), 'Vocational Preferences of School Leavers in a Scottish Industrial Area', *British Journal of Psychology*, Vol. XXIX, pp. 144-66.

PARSONS, T. (1964), *The Social System*, London, Routledge & Kegan Paul.

PEČULJIĆ, M. (1965), 'Osnove Ideje i Kritika', *Sociologija*, Vol. VII(2), pp. 197-220. (Translation available from the authors.)

PIAGET, J. (1953), *The Origin of Intelligence in the Child*, London, Routledge & Kegan Paul.

POMIANOWSKI, J. (1959), 'Mass Culture: A Case History', *Polish Perspectives*, no. 19, pp. 35-46.

POPPER, K. (1957), *The Poverty of Historicism*, London, Routledge & Kegan Paul.

RADCLIFFE-BROWN, A. (1963), *Structure and Function in Primitive Society*, London, Cohen & West.

REX, J. (1963), *Key Problems of Sociological Theory*, London, Routledge & Kegan Paul.

RHODES, R. (1968), 'The Disguised Conservatism in Evolutionary Development Theory', *Science and Society*, Vol. XXXII(4), pp. 383-412.

RIDDELL, D. (1968a), 'Social Self-Government in Yugoslavia', *British Journal of Sociology*, Vol. XIX, pp. 47-75.

RIDDELL, D. (1968b), review of 'The American Occupational Structure'. *Sociological Review*, Vol. 16(1), p. 101.

RIDDELL, D. (1969), review of 'Who Rules America', *Sociology*, Vol. 3(3), pp. 431-3.

ROSENTHAL, R. (1966), *Experimental Effects in Behavioural Research*, New York, Appleton.

RUNCIMAN, W. (1966), *Relative Deprivation and Social Justice*, London, Routledge & Kegan Paul.

SAMUEL, R. (1960), 'Dr. Abrams and the End of Politics', *New Left Review*, no. 5, pp. 2-9.

SEELEY, J. (1963), *Social Science? Some Probative Problems*, in Stein & Vidich (1963), q.v.

SHIPMAN, M. (1968), *Sociology of the School*, London, Longmans.

SILBERMAN, C. (1964), *Crisis in Black and White*, New York, Random House.

SMELSER, N. (1960), *Social Change in the Industrial Revolution*, London, Routledge & Kegan Paul.

SOSENSKY, I. (1964), *The Problem of Quality in Relation to Some Issues of Social Change*, in Zollschan and Hirsch (1964), q.v.

SPENCER, H. (1893), *Principles of Sociology, Vol. 1*, London, Williams & Norgate.

STEIN, M. & VIDICH, A., editors, (1963), *Sociology on Trial*, Englewood Cliffs, N.J., Prentice Hall.

TAWNEY, R. (1948), *Religion and the Rise of Capitalism*, Harmondsworth, Penguin.

TAYLOR, C. (1958), 'The Poverty of The Poverty of Historicism', *Universities and Left Review*, no. 4, pp. 77-78.

TAYLOR, L. & TAYLOR, I. (1968), 'We Are All Deviationists Now—Some Comments on Crime', *International Socialism*, no. 34, pp. 29-32.

THERBORN, G. (1968), 'From Petrograd to Saigon', *New Left Review*, no. 48, pp. 3-11.

THOMPSON, E. (1963), *The Making of the English Working Class*, London, Gollancz.

TROTSKY, L. (1960), *My Life*, New York, Grosset & Dunlap.

VENABLE, V. (1966), *Human Nature: The Marxian View*, New York, Meridian Books.

VENESS, T. (1962), *School Leavers: Their Aspirations and Expectations*, London, Methuen.

WEBB, J. (1962), 'The Sociology of a School', *British Journal of Sociology*, Vol. XIII(3), pp. 264-72.

WEBER, M. (1965), *The Protestant Ethic and the Spirit of Capitalism*, London, Unwin University Books.

WHYTE, L. (1949), *The Science of Culture*, New York, Grove Press.

WORLD HEALTH ORGANIZATION, (1966), *Aspects of Family Mental Health in Europe*, London, H.M.S.O., Public Health Papers.

WORSLEY, P. (1957a), 'Margaret Mead, Science or Science Fiction', *Science and Society*, Vol. XXI(2).

WORSLEY, P. (1957b), *The Trumpet Shall Sound*, London, MacGibbon & Kee.

WRONG, D. (1964), *The Oversocialized Conception of Man in Modern Sociology*, in Coser & Rosenberg (1964), q.v.

ZOLLSCHAN, G. & HIRSCH, W., editors, (1964), *Explorations in Social Change*, London, Routledge & Kegan Paul.

ZOLLSCHAN, G. & PERUCCI, R. (1964), *Social Stability and Social Process: An Initial Presentation of Relevant Categories*, in Zollschan & Hirsch (1964), q.v.